Theophylline

Erín Moure

Theophylline

an a-poretic migration via the modernisms of Rukeyser, Bishop, Grimké (*de Castro, Vallejo*)

Erín Moure

Published in Canada and the USA in 2023 by House of Anansi Press Inc.
houseofanansi.com

House of Anansi Press is committed to protecting our natural environment. This book is made of material from well-managed FSC®-certified forests, recycled materials, and other controlled sources.

House of Anansi Press is a Global Certified Accessible™ (GCA by Benetech) publisher. The ebook version of this book meets stringent accessibility standards and is available to readers with print disabilities.

27 26 25 24 23 1 2 3 4 5

Library and Archives Canada Cataloguing in Publication

Title: Theophylline : an a-poretic migration via the modernisms of
Rukeyser, Bishop, Grimké (de Castro, Vallejo) / Erín Moure.
Other titles: Poetic migration via the modernisms of Rukeyser, Bishop, Grimké (de Castro, Vallejo)
Names: Moure, Erín, 1955- author.
Description: Poems. | In the subtitle, the first "n", "a-", and "r" appear in a lighter and smaller font. |
Includes bibliographical references.
Identifiers: Canadiana (print) 20230197647 | Canadiana (ebook) 20230197663 |
ISBN 9781487011604 (softcover) | ISBN 9781487011611 (EPUB)
Classification: LCC PS8576.O96 T54 2023 | DDC C811/.54—dc23

Cover design: Alysia Shewchuk
Book design and typesetting: Marijke Friesen

House of Anansi Press is grateful for the privilege to work on and create from the Traditional Territory of many Nations, including the Anishinabeg, the Wendat, and the Haudenosaunee, as well as the Treaty Lands of the Mississaugas of the Credit.

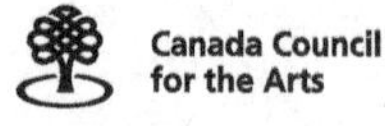

With the participation of the Government of Canada
Avec la participation du gouvernement du Canada | Canadä

We acknowledge for their financial support of our publishing program the Canada Council for the Arts, the Ontario Arts Council, and the Government of Canada.

Printed and bound in Canada

Author's Note

In this work of *essai-poetry*, occasional words of poets and theorists are quoted for purposes of critical engagement/commentary, with attribution. In addition:

This book is dedicated to the memory of Claire Harris, Caribbean-Canadian poet from Trinidad who once taught Language Arts to Calgary middle school children, from diagramming sentences to the making of paragraph and essay (this one wrote on clouds) to staging part of Macbeth *so as to experience text and space in interaction (this one carried the head of the gent in question).*

EM, Grades 7–9, 1966–69

L'air est déjà, *dans la bouche* et les poumons, la *matière* quasi organique par laquelle s'articule, s'accentue, se respire et se module le phrasé de notre parole, de notre pensée.

Georges Didi-Huberman, *Gestes d'air et de pierre*

Theophylline is pronounced: thē-ˈä-fə-lən

I walk   as my mother did
                    stoking the
fluttering

image

Claire Harris
"Of Survival"

THEOPHYLLYINE an- aporetic migration, + poems

RESPIRATIONS & RECHERCHES

HER PHARMACOPŒIA

—leaving (*to you, dear reader ...*

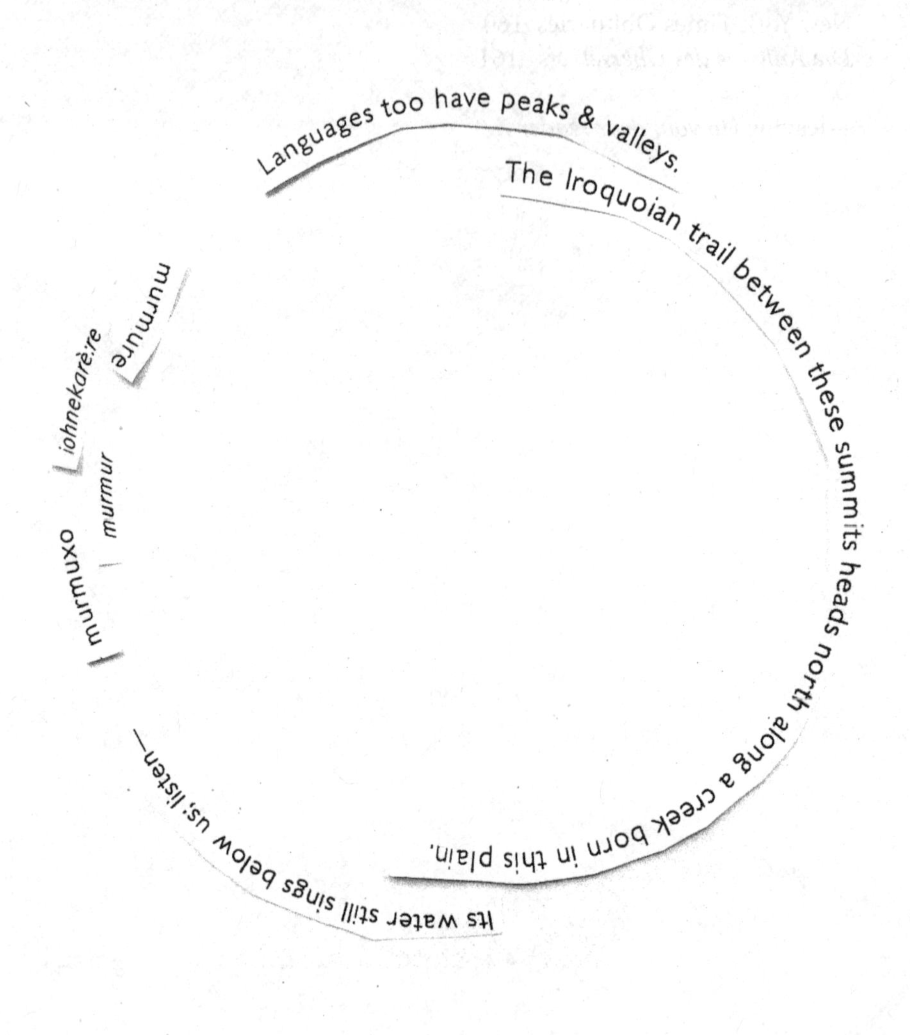
Languages too have peaks & valleys.
The Iroquoian trail between these summits heads north along a creek born in this plain.
Its water still sings below us; listen—
murmuxo
murmur
iohnekarè:re
murmure

Respirations & recherches

Such is the space where the question of modernity emerges
as a form of interrogation:
to what do I belong in this present?

Homi Bhabha, *The Location of Culture*

Inhale / Écoute

(time's threshold)

To the Woodberry Poetry Room and its archives of voices I came as foreigner and translator of poetry to think on beauty and space (for the Room is beautiful) and (the ache of) migration, wanting to attend to three things:

- The process of hearing a voice
- The place where the voice is heard
- The impulse to make a poem instead of …
  something else.

17 April 2017
Cambridge, MA

A silence now, audible. In the noise of no noise, the test pattern static noise of the inside of the head. And,

in the chest, the sound of breathing.
Rales, we called them.
Rales in the chest. Their stutter
audible in the breath.
Rhonchi.

We are organisms in which breathing-space and breathing-time are not guaranteed.

Asthma names me, has always named me.

I am small and in bed and I can only breathe with great wheezing difficulty. Pillows prop me and I am wearing pyjamas.

It is 1959 or 1960 and asthma medications are not yet very good.

Wood and light.

The first poetry I know is *Mother Goose* and A. A. Milne's *When We Were Very Young* and *Now We Are Six*. Like Christopher Robin, I too have sneezles and wheezles, but I am never better the next day.

Coughing and not-coughing. Light and a tree outside, not a tree, a bush, a lilac bush. Wheeze. Pædiatrician Dr. Alan Cody comes from his home or his offices in the Greyhound Building to Altadore to give me injections and, for a few hours after these home visits and quiet talks with my mother, breathing is eased and I can let myself be carried away by the sound of voices outside or elsewhere in the house.

Listening. The patter of voices elsewhere in the house. In the Room, the three women American modernist poets whose works/voices I have chosen to open myself to: all have in some way a relation to *elsewheres*. Thus *translation*. An elsewhere of nearly forbidden light:

To expose my Being to their voices in the Wood and Light of the Room. We say we are hearing a 'Voice' but is it not the Breath making this Voice, and who can breathe? who speak? who listen? I breathe and listen: how and with what Text or Articulation will I Respond?

All three poets have made migrations, are formed by elsewheres they touched or inhabited, and each has been marked as 'questionable' in some way—gender, sexuality, race—by the socius in and through which they vanish and appear.

Over nine days in the Room, I try to discern the forms (what's still), grasp the contrasting shapes (what moves) in the poetry of Muriel Rukeyser, Elizabeth Bishop and Angelina Weld Grimké. In the United States of America in 2017 at Harvard in the Woodberry Poetry Room, I arrive across a border to apprehend an American poetry of the 20th century as a translator might approach works in another tongue.

To intend English from a foreign English, and a foreign time.
To attune to a minor language (Kafka, Deleuze). To *listen*. Breathe.

Then I didn't write anything new in poetry for over three years.

I begin much later,

in fits and starts,

stutters in the confinement of the pandemic.
The public gone. And Elisa S., excising my poems
& inserting hers, interferes again in my work,
completely ignoring what I was desiring.

What am I desiring?
Can a poem (like silence) listen?
Can breath listen?

Something Else

Elisa Sampedrín

Whose muse was "lost   jostle
cause" but
cause nonetheless

as when the bright square on
the opposite wall
is "light's shadow"

as if "shadow" and
"reflection" were synony*mal*

herself marauder too
though peaceable

never holds ever verily

orphan is child yet of
Orpheus

"they" of song

ferment solidarity grammar dissolve

A dissolve and flutter. Since my mother died (16y 6m 22d), I've had difficulty writing poetry. You'd never know it. I still live in and love poetry. Yet her death leaves a scab on poetry's tempest. No new skin emerges, the scab mercifully stays.

Instead, poets keep me alive in their poems, as I translate and live with their words in my mouth. The light square on the wall opposite is really ('truly') light's shadow. Elisa Sampedrín interferes. Thanks to my brother, I take self-defence, learn to repel multiple attackers. I paste a young Dad over a still of Giorgio Agamben (so wrong about the pandemic) from Pasolini's 1964 biblical epic *Il vangelo secondo Matteo*, its time stamp visible so any reader of *The Elements* can gaze at the young philosopher on YouTube.

Then to America I go, for America harbours my translations when Canada will not (international poetry, ineligible for funding, is almost entirely ignored by Canadian publishers). I ache to read sounds, to let voices inhabit me. Translating Rosalía de Castro, early Galician modernist we never had in English, has altered my ears' capacities. I want to translate American modernism in these ears by fiercely vibrating in the swell of their syllables. Through their words and voices I find poetry not as 'my poetry' but as poetry's corollary: *her listener*

Orphan is child of
Orpheus
Orpheu

A dweller in curiosity. What emerges is yet 'to be drawn.' For what are we but
"not innocent"
In-innocent and
not bystanders

Wherever I go, I want to listen to women's voices. They charm the animals and make the trees dance. King of Thrace and Calliope, you could have had no better children than Muriel, Elizabeth, Angelina. Oh Orpheu. *Orfa eu. Perdida son eu (os meus eus) en ti.*

MR

Bronx, New York City, 1913–Upper East Side, NYC, 1980

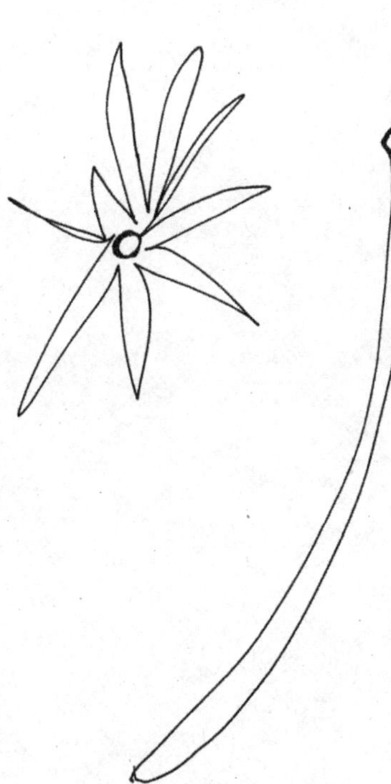

from "Then"

When I am dead, even then
I am still listening to you.
I will still be making poems for you
out of silence;
silence will be falling into that silence,
it is building music.

Do I move toward form, do I use all my fear?

Muriel Rukeyser
"Double Ode"

Muriel Rukeyser's migrations take her incessantly outward and back, to zones of resistance to Capital and returning to the soil of Capital's most iconic formulation: America. Reporter, documentarist, seeker of Justice, she brings back the news via a rhythmic poetic in which phrase/sentence cohere yet punctuation and spacing defy coherence in order to extend it. Her poetry calls forth. It is a rhetoric. Unflinching.

In 1932, 19-year-old Rukeyser attends the Scottsboro trials as a Vassar journalist and gets typhoid fever when briefly jailed for "fraternizing with African Americans." She writes of Black miners driven to silicosis working unprotected on the Hawks Nest Tunnel in W. Virginia, is in Spain at the outbreak of Civil War in 1936, witness to the community anarchism (self-help and fraternity not chaos) of Barcelona, refuses to pay taxes in 1968 to reject US involvement in Vietnam, is in Hanoi in 1972 during the endless Vietnam War to protest US bombings, returns to lie down in protest on the Senate floor in Washington, is arrested. In South Korea in 1974 (head of PEN America), she keeps vigil for days at the gates of the prison holding Kim Chi Ha (sentenced to death for the crime of poetry) to demand his release. In 1978, one of her last poetry readings, a mini-stroke topples her and she reads from the floor in a tangle of mic and wires, refusing an ambulance.

Her home is America, site of justice and compassion. If its government and courts serve injustice, R. raises voice and body in revolt. Her sexuality is enacted not declared: she loves wo/men; she raises her son on her own. Her longest relationship is her last, with her agent Monica McCall, 24 years her elder, who outlived her by two years.

Since the 1970s I have ~~mis~~remembered a Kim poem as "Food is heaven, rice is heaven; when we eat rice, we take heaven into ourselves." 밥이 하늘입니다 actually says something like: "Rice is heaven; food is heaven; we must share heaven for we can't reach it alone; eat rice together; rice is as are stars in the sky." Not a good start as a ~~rememberer~~ translator … though in 1974 it was often impossible to find versions of Korean poems in English, and even on finding, hard to find the name of their translator …

밥이 입으로 들어갈 때에
하늘을 몸속에 모시는 것
밥은 하늘입니다
https://www.youtube.com/watch?v=HoM1cEYTKIM

Mellifluous

Elisa Sampedrín

What then is mellifluous
that honeyed voice
or flow

Calliope's inner membrane
I was born from
Orphic

darkness
thrashing in the woods at night

(it's just the dog
someone threw him a shoe : hey

that's my ~~shoe!~~

~~organism~~
~~cockroach~~
poem

Child of my mother, I might have been American, if not for the *Immigration Act 1924* that forbade her family's return in 1929 to Cleveland's mills (oh Rexroth's *orange bears*) from the Ukrainian fields and hills where they'd gone back in 1921 at war's end, due to the illness of my grandma's father. America: why did you not want us back?

Rukeyser
listening to her 'Bronx accent' (they say)

Laconic but insistent, her voice. In my 1960s awakening (child in Calgary, a city then 10% American) during the struggles against US colonial wars on 'communism,' few US poets exemplify protest better than Muriel Rukeyser. She is for me the inheritor of the Wilfred Owen I'd read in school, of Jeffers and his "Shine, Perishing Republic."

To her I looked, to a woman poet who does not address her readers as 'boys' (as did Jeffers, shutting me out). Hers is another address:

> What if one woman told the truth about her life?
> The world would split open
>
> "Käthe Kollwitz"
> *The Speed of Darkness*, 1968

The complexity of 'witnessing' is her solidity. But through what eyes does she witness? Who reads and why?

The clamour of her forms that wrestle—as they display—the perils of sincerity. What does anyone see? Our own framework blinds us

~~*thrashing in the woods at night*~~

a shoe!

R.'s is a voracious and loquacious line, many lines many poems, 515 published, to my count. She trusts something called experience. "Poetry," Rukeyser says, "is making something out of experience, and giving it out to someone."

This experience is 'one's own' which is not *all* of experience. It struggles against and with the experience of the other.

*when she must, she does say she is a 'tourist'

She has to come 'home' and 'give it out to someone,' not just 'give it to someone.' The latter implies a one-to-one personal relationship, but the former, giving it out, implies people are a crowd, and though you claim you share with them, they share with you, in fact you don't know what or if they are ready to receive. This is the poetry of witness (wherein who positions who? who is silent/ced?)

The energy expended is all yours.
She expends her energy,
gives it out.

Even when arrested (Scottsboro), stopped by the police (Washington), standing at the prison gates (Seoul):
she breathes freely.

NB: This free *breath* does not always grant her *voice*. In her last 15 years, often in stroke recovery, her giving-out is a "code of pauses" where silences "are part of the sound" (*The Life of Poetry: 1949, 1974, 1997*, 116–17): she battles aphasia, recognizes the gravity in grave and the art in artifact: *Speak to you then?*

> I believe in poetry. I believe that the life of people and the life of poetry must ultimately mean the same thing ... I believe in the life of the spirit generally walking the earth, against war, against slavery, for the giving of all the processes and art and technique of living.
>
> to *Louis Untermeyer*, 1940
> (R.'s declaration)

That Rukeyser is white is—crucial to the success of her enterprise: in her era, the experience ('giving it out') of a non-'racialized' person automatically has perceived value. In such a paradigm, a white person is taken as speaking on behalf of, and to, all. *Compassion* semi-automatically accrues to her. *Insight* accrues to her. She never has to struggle to speak in *her own* voice to give out what is perceived as *plurality's* truth.

Even though a *woman*, a *lover of women*, a *Jew*, a *single mother* are conditions encumbered by prejudice and misogyny in America, Rukeyser can assume the rostrum. Wind in her hair. She steps off the plane in Barcelona, in Hanoi. She clears her throat and looks outward.

Her voice is certain, sure. Her face "heart-shaped" (Kinnell).

Falling just short of the evangelical (an American harbour), her documentary voice is clamour yet insists on clarity. The 'productive ambiguity' that is part of poetry's power is pared away in exchange for this 'clarity.' Her audience is 'out there,' or 'here,' listening. Or is yet unborn ...

Is listening 'witness'? Is the emotion of poetry 'plural,' or is it just in 'me'? *Why do I see 'whiteness' in 'witness'?*

R.'s voice is like oratory: what is oratory? Speech that frames us so we make ourselves heard. Speech intended for 'witnesses.' The witnessing of speech. But who witnesses what? Who witnesses this speech of the poet?

*Seebe.**

---

* "And I knew, from his look when we picked him up and went into the train: you could tell he'd never been in a train before. So then it's just me constructing something. And for what, to make me the author of the piece? I realized that I pulled him into the emptiness of the poem. The poem was the real emptiness." On "Seebe" (written 1985) in *My Beloved Wager* (1999).

The vast emptiness.

The poem has fallen apart into mere description.
It is years later, thinking of the mind's assumptive power & remembering
the train hitting the boy at Seebe, Alberta & how I went out
to get him. Here we have only my assumptions, only the arrogance of
Erin Mouré made into the poem; in the course of history, which is
description, the boy is mute. We have no way of entering into his images
now. The description itself, even if questioned, portrays the arrogance
of the author. In all claims to the story, there is muteness. The writer as
witness, speaking the stories, is a lie, a liberal bourgeois lie. Because the
speech is the writer's speech, and each word of the writer robs the
witnessed of their own voice, muting them.

Lifting him up, bone weary, taking him
into the vast, vast emptiness.

from "Seebe," in *WSW* (1989)

I think of *conditions of reception*. Rukeyser does know that these exist (she faces up to Senator McCarthy and his anti-communist inquisitors; she insists the reader is essential to the poem), yet she is more passionately involved in *production*. 'Giving it out' is a loquacity. The giving is, to her, crucial to the reception, but herein lies an illusion about reception never fully examined. Though she believes the poem exists because a reception is possible via readers or listeners, to my knowledge, she never questions publicly who and how the listener is able to receive her words. Her listener is assumed to be like her in class, race, and condition of hunger (I wonder) ...

Who is receiving? Who listens?

Who reads MR today?

Her work testifies to social responsibility, an enduring part of Judaic tradition. For R., life is a gift (gratuitous, as Chus Pato would say) meant to be inhabited/enacted consciously every moment in a response to the world and others, and this responsiveness *is* a praise. To make the broken world less broken, R. nurtures Justice and the Virtues in her own socius: *America.*

In a way, she addresses not *these* readers, *these* listeners, she addresses America.* As HaShem, perhaps. As *Nadie.* As go^{d}.

Who can speak, or not speak, is unexamined, elided. As it is (by and large) in later poetry called of 'witness.' R. does not witness, she rhetoricizes; at least she seems to take on and acknowledge this role of rhetoric that speaks on behalf of all (unexamined).

Like Whitman, who drew his rhythms from his body and the sea, she articulates "the relation of our breathing

to our heartbeat."

**but what is this America? Whose is? Who breathes?*

The insistence of R.'s voice is a rhetoric
that opens sound and word together
in penetrating and resonant complicity. With this voice
you are safe, listener, in its gravity and generosity
the you, and me, are safe;
history speaks 'us' and we 'speak to history'
Nor is sexuality absent in her lines, "the prick
and cunt," nor birth for "sons
fall burning into Asia"
(but what is R.'s Asia)
(a word)
(foreign/unknown/sexed)_does she gives us this word 'Asia'
to speak of *American* sons in Vietnam? *They* burnt?

For Asia already has its sons who on their ground
do speak—but not in Rukeyser's poem;
that poem inhabits and sustains *empire*,
even in its speaking an Empire sustains its accent
and she prepares it all the sky, and a continent
(I
reject this)

"Children burning in the catacombs"
"Before we were wounds, we were houses"
I wrote those lines
I quote from no one

Asia is a comfort to me
Asia in my mother's eyes not East but West without memory,
curtained from Europe

Before we are joy, we were a
humility that was not humiliation

Landing in the boats (numbers pinned upon the children's coats)
Oh heart

~~but in listening~~
~~Rukeyser's cadences enact us~~
~~with her we ride a chariot across the sun~~

Rukeyser on TV (
there is also *this* strug/gle
)
Camera Three in 1965 w. poets James Dickey, Peter Viereck,
host James MacAndrew

PV interrupts MR constantly, at volume, a logorrhea, and squirms endlessly in his chair with arms darting outward, occupying not just aural space but visual, and making it hard to grasp what MR is trying to say

MR says:
"the general nervousness about poetry"

MR says:
"the desire for love, the desire for form"

MR says of poetry:
"an effort at speech"

The three men talk over her and she has a hard time getting a word in edgewise

MR at 15:53:
"I am impossible, I cannot exist, women poets can't exist …"

MR at 19:10 when asked to read, reads part 12 of "The Outer Banks":
"the edge of experience"
"women, ships, lost voices"

Her determination to recuperate histories of the marginalized that would otherwise be lost …

Flying to Hanoi

Muriel Rukeyser, scratched by ES

~~I thought I was going to the poets, but I am~~
~~going to the children.~~
~~I thought I was going to the children, but I am~~
~~going to the women.~~
~~I thought I was going to the women, but I am~~
~~going to the fighters.~~
~~I thought I was going to the fighters, but I am~~
~~going to the men and women who are inventing peace.~~
~~I thought I was going to the inventors of peace, but I am~~
~~going to the poets.~~
My life is flying to your life.

Du mußt dein Leben ändern.
R. M. Rilke, "Archaïscher Torso Apollos"
(unanswered, or answered with a shoe, or *zoco galego*)

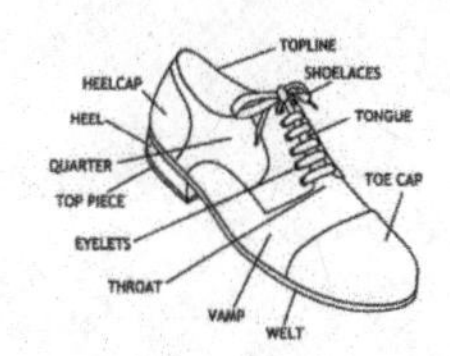

She is "the excessive ancestor of Adrienne Rich," wrote Eileen Myles in 1997 in *The Nation*, reviewing the reissue of Rukeyser's 1949 book *The Life of Poetry*; "the book is chock-full of radiant abstractions." I am unsure if this is a compliment.

The emotional charge of the poem is what R. lays claim to. I turn back to the poems. "Letter to the Front" invokes her sense of responsibility, potent in the long shadow cast by the wars of the 20th century.

To be a Jew in the twentieth century
Is to be offered a gift. If you refuse,
Wishing to be invisible, you choose
Death of the spirit, the stone insanity.
Accepting, take full life. Full agonies:
Your evening deep in the labyrinthine blood
Of those who resist, fail, and resist ...

She arrives at last at the women:

Surely it is time for the true grace of women
Emerging, in their lives' colors, from the rooms, from the harvests,
From the delicate prisons, to speak their promises.

Finally, when the poem ends, the *I* begins, giving it out:

I now send you, for a beginning, praise.

Rukeyser is among the first to bring young Octavio Paz into English. The two met in Berkeley in 1944, and in 1948 R. includes six of his poems in *The Green Wave* with a note saying they are by Paz *and* herself (surprise: usually attributed solely to MR). She is modest, calls her translations "adaptations." Into Paz's long exhalation, she builds a beautiful exchange of sounds that emit rhetorical flourishes. Her poem falls and rises, syncopates with lexicon (blackness instead of darkness; *she* is blind, not just *her feet*). Her punctuation marks text with pausal spacings; punctuation bears semantic force. I marvel at her version for its visuality, its Rukeyser marking Paz.

Street—Octavio Paz, tr. EM

It's a street long and quiet.
I walk in darkness and trip and fall
and rise up and tread footblind
on mute stones and dry leaves
that behind me someone else treads:
if I tarry, they tarry;
if I run, they run. I turn my face: no one.
All is dark and dead ends,
and I turn round and around at corners
that just lead back into the street
where no one awaits or follows me,
where I follow a man who trips
and rises up and says upon seeing me: no one.

La Calle—Octavio Paz

Es una calle larga y silenciosa.
Ando en tinieblas y tropiezo y caigo
y me levanto y piso con pies ciegos
las piedras mudas y las hojas secas
y alguien detrás de mí también las pisa:
si me detengo, se detiene;
si corro, corre. Vuelvo el rostro: nadie.
Todo está oscuro y sin salida,
y doy vueltas y vueltas en esquinas
que dan siempre a la calle
donde nadie me espera ni me sigue,
donde yo sigo a un hombre que tropieza
y se levanta y dice al verme: nadie.

The Street—tr. MR in *The Green Wave*, 1948

Here is a long and silent street.
I walk in blackness and I stumble and fall
and rise, and I walk blind, my feet
trampling the silent stones and the dry leaves.
Someone behind me also tramples, stones, leaves:
if I slow down, he slows;
if I run, he runs.   I turn   :   nobody.
Everything dark and doorless,
only my steps aware of me,
I turning and turning among these corners
which lead forever to the street
where nobody waits for, nobody follows me,
where I pursue a man who stumbles
and rises and says when he sees me   :   nobody.

To Paz's "sin salida," *without exit*, Rukeyser ventures *doorless*. Is it her American optimism? *Doorless* says a wall without egress; applied to a street, *doorless* may mean its passage lies open. To Paz's "sigo," *I follow*, an act free of aggression, Rukeyser has *pursuit*. His verb "pisar," *to step on*, in Rukeyser, *tramples*. And she adds an extra line not in Paz: "only my steps aware of me"—to make her 1948 version sonnet-length? Or did Paz later remove a line from his?

A kind of terror and panic rises more quickly to the surface in R. than it does in OP or in EM. Yet it rises via a restraint, here not-loquacious. And its final note: R.'s poem ends not with "one" negated (as in EM, a total absence), but with "body" negated, which is to say, present.

Rukeyser's own work is far from passive. It engages the materiality of propellers, bombs, blades, mirrors, planes, fireworks. It seems at times to echo something opposite to the impulse of freedom that her words continuously advocate: futurism, that proto-Fascist and masculinist European praise of modernity and speed and virility.

Rukeyser is virile in her loquacity. And I listen to this virile voice and documentary promise.

I listen to the unpouring of this accent, its incessant hold. Its spacing and extension of vowels and rising tonalities. And always she talks of *form** as if of *futures*

If a street has no doors, *perhaps we can enter its great arch (when R. falls silent)*
and walk right through ...

~~nobody~~ shoe

**she uses this word on 60 pages of her collected poems, says googlebooks*

I read and reread a tiny OP poem whose syntax makes it hard to render in English without losing a shimmer of doubled meanings. Rukeyser rhetoricizes, adds *death* and *eyes* and causation (*how*). She repeats to capture both senses of *verdadero*: 1) true, 2) real. Yet the original holds an even more crucial doubling resonance: at once a *lying-life of truths* and *a lying life-of-truths*. Rukeyser dodges this productive ambiguity in 1948 to deploy the clarity she values.

Epitafio para un poeta, OP

Quiso cantar, cantar
para olvidar
su vida verdadera de mentiras
y recordar
su mentirosa vida de verdades.

Poet's Epitaph, MR (in *The Green Wave*, 1948)

He sang until his death
singing to close his eyes
to his true life, his real life of lies;
and to remember till he died
how it had lied, his unreal life of truth.

Epitaph by a Poet (g-neutral), EM

They wished to sing, sing
to forget
their true life of lies
and to bring to mind
their lying life of truths.

Verisimilitude for Rukeyser, ES

She wanted to sing, sing
to abolish
her veritable life of lies
and to polish
her lying life of verities.

In the Woodberry Poetry Room, ears transfixed by the gravelled consonants and lengthened vowels of Rukeyser's oration, I balk at the sincerity of 'witnessing' in poetry without engaging the conditions of reception that make listening possible.

To 'witness' is to bear the weight and agony of a heard story into your core, so that your next acts are infused and altered. As in Rilke witnessing the torso of Apollo. Not flying to the life of another, not appropriating a story into your own speech, but to realize—in a *realization* that is *act accomplished in action*—: "you must change your life."

Rukeyser restlessly keeps speaking. The public feels a *soulagement*. A recognition, but who then acts? Who *realizes*?

Rukeyser: "I am working out the vocabulary of my silences"

"the shape of the body speaking its evidence"

"who will speak these days if not me, if not you?"

Du mußt dein Leben ändern.
Rilke, "Archaïscher Torso Apollos"
(still unanswered) (the vocabulary of silences: the 'something' else?)

PLEASE BELIEVE THE PUNCTUATION.
(she stamped on submissions to warn editors to leave punctuation alone)

If there were no witness but the language of the poem, what would the ears scent? Where would the place of the reader be? What ancient torso's silence of form?

(smells)

Elisa Sampedrín

cement in the wet gutter
won't go down well

smell of wet winter boots
is not the same

as spring gum boots from
the garden

one of us is still there so
don't even ask

there are no smells in poetry

ink maybe, hot persons in their winter
coats wet from the blizzard

arrived to go quiet
at the poetry reading

not knowing their coats stink

and history
won't remind them (the tape deck)

So I upend my own reception: start to read Elizabeth Bishop while listening on headphones to Rukeyser, as if to *rukeyser* Bishop (who hated speeches and poetry readings—'giving it out' was not hers). With her taut images in juxtaposition, EB enables a shimmer to emerge between registers and linguistic glints, visual shifts of presences. In the gaps, chinks that she devises,

the incommensurate or inexpressible glows.

Then invert my experiment: read Muriel Rukeyser while listening to Bishop on the tape deck, a *voix serrée* fiercely clashing with Rukeyser's inscriptive expansiveness. Impossible to read R.'s sprawling *escritura* in a restrained aural space. I can't *bishop* R. Sampedrín is right: *no smell.*

~~Epitaph for Bishop, EM~~

~~She sang, sang so she~~
~~could seem to forget~~
~~her veritable life of lies~~
~~and seem to remember~~
~~her lying life of truths.~~

~~or, simply, a condensation with the sound of birds/flowers/water:~~

~~"Let truth lie."~~

Shoe for E. Sampedrín, by Herself

She sang off-key sang

wah forget it.

Her ring of truth brings life to lie

and faux reggret it:

her lying life sings t/rue.

As/thma. Talk now about breathlessness?

EB

Worcester, MA, 1911 (Great Village, NS)–Boston, MA, 1979

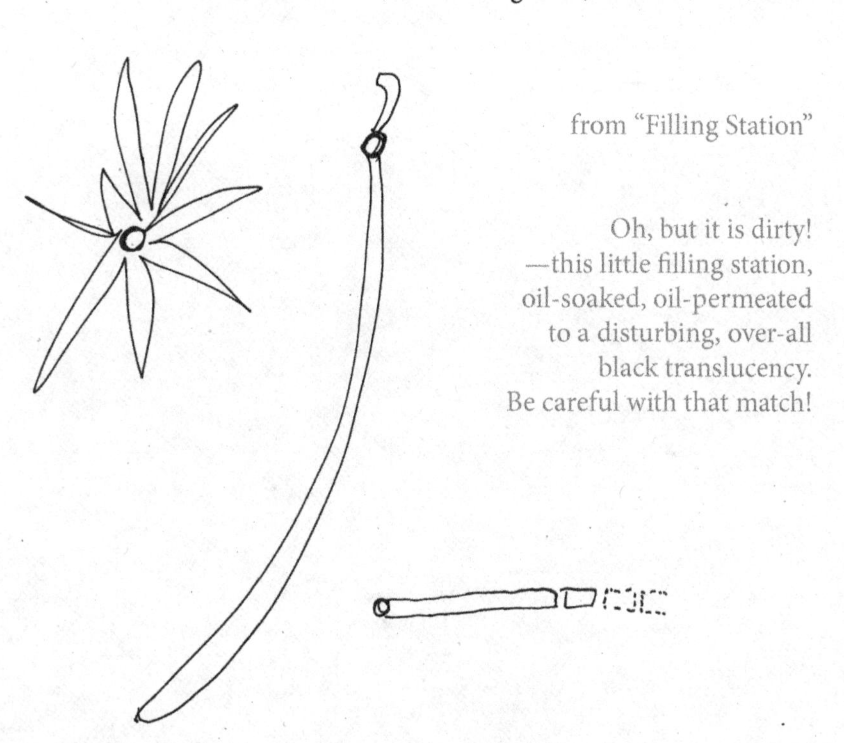

from "Filling Station"

Oh, but it is dirty!
—this little filling station,
oil-soaked, oil-permeated
to a disturbing, over-all
black translucency.
Be careful with that match!

I'm practically cured, but so full of adrenaline, morphine, and a particularly drugged and poisonous kind of cough syrup, that I am light-headed and …

1 January 1935, EB letter to Frani Blough, on asthma

Elizabeth Bishop's migration was one long loop south from a Boston/ NYC axis to Brazil, with fleeting small loops north to Nova Scotia's Fundy shores, and finally a return to Boston. Hers did not come from a stable site called 'home,' or return to home, nor did it speak out to a socius, a social centre of responsibility to and in the world. It left outward familiarity so she could thrive. In Brazil, she inscribed place/ motion, saturation/scattering, rupture/connection, village/family, *marais*/birds for readers who came to her poems in English,

while she faced tropical forest, misty steeps, perilous roads, heat, mixed with (though never at ease in conversation, she insisted) the Portuguese of aristocratic friends, workers and house servants, and with politics and corruption, despair and hope, and poems.

Her titles mark a trajectory—*North and South, Questions of Travel, Geography III*—along with melded north-south seasons of *A Cold Spring*.

Her reticence is famed. Did Elizabeth Bishop 'avoid' self-description, as some say? Or: a-void it.* Were her descriptions "desperate," as Colm Tóibín claimed, imputing psychological motives to her inscriptions? Whose interest is served by imputing an internal psychological state—desperation—to EB? Hers was perhaps a *despiration*. "Water but also air," Octavio Paz noted. Her arduous patience at not being able to breathe in the world (asthma merits panic, but panic makes it worse, thus patience). Moments, hours, nights, weeks. Asthma wears at the body. Impossible to 'give it out' if you can hardly breathe.

You give it in, inward.

No tourist-reporter, Bishop moved in her migrations as tourist-exile, able to articulate a discomfort that still speaks to our 21st century condition. *Shouldn't we just stay home?*

The question's rhetorical. To her, there was no home, or if there were home how did we come to be in it, and why is it marked by a scream?

Smells in Bishop: pickles, coffee, carpets, motor oil (*upholstery grime*
Her perspectives (wires, coffee, balcony, bread, moth-flight-tear

To Bishop, poetry dealt with a problem, not an experience: "My maternal grandmother had a glass eye ... often it looked heavenward, or off at an angle, while the real eye looked at you. Off and on I have written out a poem called 'Grandmother's Glass Eye' which should be about the problem of writing poetry. The situation of my grandmother strikes me as rather like the situation of the poet: the difficulty of combining the real with the decidedly unreal; the natural with the unnatural; the curious effect a poem produces of being as normal as *sight* and yet as synthetic, as artificial, as a *glass eye*."

Asthmatic, Bishop mentioned not breathing or smelling but seeing: a *glass eye* that sees sidelong in silence (sigh.lens)

[Her grandmother: B.'s compass after her dad's death and dear mom's breakdown/vanishing into an asylum when B. was five. At seven, she was taken from her maternal g's by her paternal g's to Boston; to them, village life was provincial, shabby. Yet to me, in rich Mi'kmaw lands—marshes salt and fresh, apple trees, red clam beaches, tides—B.'s village home and school were solidly middle-class. In Boston: no more chow-chows or affectionate cooking but yes, asthma. Much worse asthma.]

So to B. poetry had less to do with breath and was more like an eye that speaks (if but to sigh). "The 'famous eye' will now put on her glasses."*

Bishop to me is a materialist poet, a lyricist (i.e. of direct address to a singularity, not a rhetor speaking to an illusory All) whose devotion to the gaps and errors—the 'quasi,' the lyric 'remainder'—in poetic address and architecture was mischevious, and deft.

Still, her "famous eye": in May 1969, amid mass protest against the US war in Vietnam, FBI surveillance of the women's liberation movement, during and after the endless struggle for civil rights, after the political assassinations, of which she said nothing, was the eye really open, or ... *glass*?

Asthma "keeps you up," a euphemism for wakefulness. You see animals and faces in the shadows. Your own animal cannot breathe, and tilts. Asthma medication, especially the early stuff, caused nervousness, palpitations, crazy nightmares when you did sleep: at least breath was easier. At times there were aural creaks in the night that seemed to be in the house but were in the head: later and adult, I'd startle at a night-time noise, while E. the cat kept sleeping.

Maybe the cat is a memory of my mother the nurse, caring for me.

(she returns here later, out of place as usual, *you'll see*)

At best I was sleeping.

Or lying face down over the edge of bed with head draped in a towel, inhaling hot vapours from a kettle on a hotplate, to loosen congestion enough to free the rales and cough up phlegm, then breathe more freely

all alone
in the wood and light of the room
(the voices elsewhere)

cadence/~~impudence~~

Pyjamas: An Essay on Childhood with Asthma

Erín Moure

We all wore our pyjamas out in those days,* wore them till the buttons fell away from what remained of the cloth. Fabrics pretty much had to disintegrate before they were replaced.

It was a serious thing to wear your pyjamas all day; you couldn't see your friends in pyjamas. You couldn't go outside. You were unseeable.

You could lie down in bed and listen to your brothers outside the house with the neighbour kids throwing the football on the lawns (an inner suburb, 1960s …).

My favourite dressing gown had buttons instead of wrapping, and was quilted, cotton, white with red stylized cats on it, and red piping.

I felt modern and safe in the favourite dressing gown. It was not a bathrobe but a dressing gown. A sign of sophistication passed down through the ages even though, in fact, I didn't feel at all well.

The sound of children playing up and down the front lawns on the street, after dinner. My bedroom window was at the front of the house. The voices sounded like a future I wanted to believe in.

It is a lonely thing, this asthma. You learn to be alone. My mother gave me the dressing gown with red cats on it. It is my best-remembered item of clothing from my childhood. There is no photo of it.

The other clothing I remember from photos, or when I see photos.

The pyjamas were already thin and worn through at the elbows and the bottoms were held up by the drawstrings as the elastic waistband had long gone slack.

"I went to school off and on, but remember chiefly lying in bed wheezing and reading …" Bishop to Anne Stevenson, 6 March 1964. *My own memories (from around the time EB wrote those words) are the same.*

It must have come from a department store, that dressing gown, there must have been many of them manufactured identically, hundreds, all over Canada and maybe further. I've looked all over the internet for an image of this dressing gown but it seems not to have survived.

It lies outside the archive.
Breath is archived, yes.
But not non-breath.

When I started to get better, I could put on my dressing gown over my pyjamas and come and sit again with them at the dinner table in the kitchen and eat my mother's food, a bit of it, and see them, my brothers and father, my mother. Their lives had moved on and mine had not. I remembered a life like this though and was glad to be permitted to visit it.

The archive is a constructed memory. It is how the future as imagined from a present desires to see the past. Its past. It is how the imagined future desires.

I could not imagine a future thus an archive was for me impossible.

So I borrow here the archives of others. What am I describing, I wonder. Myself? A self?

A dressing gown with red piping and red cats on it.

How can any poet be responsible to a socius, see life as gift, and her task in life as a praise that might mend the broken, when she can't breathe? Bishop was sickly as a child in Nova Scotia and much worse in Boston where asthma and eczema kept her schooled at home until nearly high school.

Not to breathe. How the nights are long!

ES: Faint taste of hard
pear
sliced and cooked soft
into oat porridge

The tree
"pereira"

Its fruit gone wild as wood
Cooked it is a chutney

air spiced with
parking lot

Air behind an avenue

Morning comes. Morning's centurion is simply light. Measuring each increment of light as height and breath. The avenue is imaginary and you can hear cars on it, the air is further off and you have to reach it to breathe ...

Bishop, unlike Rukeyser, was grounded in an ontology, not an ethics (no Levinas here, or yes, Levinas: the face of the stranger is present and dear, yet off-kilter). Ontology's primacy makes sense when you cannot breathe, when, in a minute or hour, you might not be able to breathe. And when you are never 'at home.' Bishop's was a perceiving self, Cartesian: she was an Elizabeth; she *heard* an '*oh* of pain' from the dentist's waiting room and realized it was (surprise or ambiguity) not her aunt's but her own voice, therefore she *was*.

Whose breath made that cry in the waiting room? *her aunt's? hers?* All those words are, to me, an agony.

Either way, she *heard* (her aunt's voice): *being* as *sonorous*: BREATH.

Her (famed) accuracy was 'liberal,' I think, for when the poem required her to fuse truths, she did so with "uncontorted intentionalness," as Marianne Moore wrote. Such a contorted phrase to describe the intensity of making the balances and tensile dis-equilibrium of a poem! In repudiating contortion, Moore might've said 'direct intentionality' but no, to be accurate, her claim to B.'s lack of contortion had in itself to contort!

The rational considering quality in her work is its strength—assisted by unwordiness, uncontorted intentionalness, the flick of impudence, the natural unforced ending ...
from "Archaically New," Moore's intro to *Trial Balances: An Anthology of New Poetry*, 1935

As breath contorts. Air. *Poems that breathe and feel*, said Paz of B. Can breath feel? Asthma numbs, narrows.

When theophylline (tea/cocoa/kola leaf extract used 1922–1980s) was ineffective in relieving Bishop's asthma in the 1940s, there was epinephrine from a glass syringe or nebulized in a device of blown glass and rubber. Or asthma cigarettes containing belladonna. They sped the heart rate and agitated you, you lay still all afternoon watching sunlight cross the wall while your heart beat fast but you could breathe. The relief of being able to breathe.

Theophylline. *Quibron*. Then cortisone injected or by mouth: brute assault that puffs you up, leaches calcium from bones. But breathe.

Nebulizing inhalers came in the 1950s, at first accessible only to those who could afford specialists and new medicines. Bishop's letters spoke of even earlier inhaler set-ups: sulphate cartridges to which she was hooked "like Carroll's caterpillar to a hookah." Ventolin came later, ubiquitous blue relief inhaler of late 20th century asthmatics. And inhaled corticosteroids. Really all just a version of this:

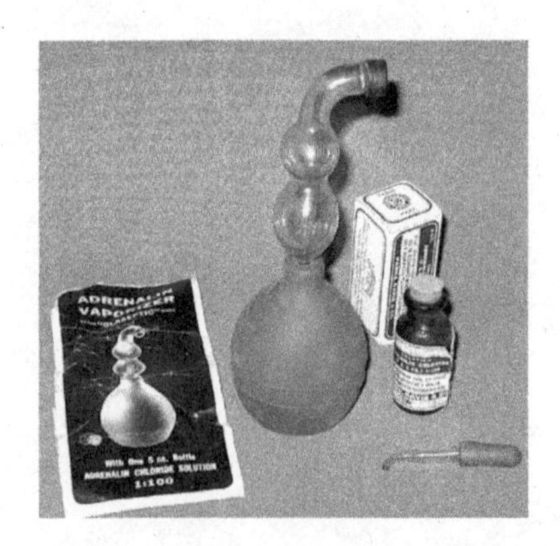

(Pharmacies ran short of Ventolin (salbutamol) during the first wave of Covid-19. Though I didn't use relief inhalers any more but a modern long-acting β_2 adrenergic receptor agonist, it was frightening to think of the viral emergency depriving asthmatics of access to medication we need every minute every day to breathe.)

I remember in every detail the texture of the paint on the wall behind my pillow. Oh life, you are sweet!

Bishop's migration: one long arc, with repeated short skips north. Headed south 'around' the Americas in 1951, a celebrated poet at 40, she disembarked the freighter in Santos, Brazil, nearly died from eating cashew fruit, stayed for care and remained 16 years in the hills north of Rio at her lover Lota de Soares's estate, or in L.'s Rio apartment in Leme above Copacabana beach.

An inheritance (and from 1951, a first-refusal contract with *The New Yorker* that paid by the line, 25% over regular rate—they also clinched her a grant for her trip to Brazil) meant Bishop, if careful, did not have to seek work to pay rent and eat till late in life. The inheritance was all she had of a father, who'd died when she was eight months old. In Brazil she lived as a lesbian, or is that even possible? It was the 1950s. She lived her lesbian life without speaking it directly, a status possible to a white woman of means with well-placed friends of means. Brazil a more forgiving place than New England. A different interface and threshold. Bishop's social conscience, unlike Rukeyser's, was not a public *rhetoric*; she did, I think, see past that of the class that welcomed her, though without discomfitting them. She had affection for servants and workers—in the kitchen with them, making cakes and Scotian pickles, she had her most natural conversations in Portuguese. Still, her poems of sympathy for ordinary Brazilians resonate to me of a class disdain, learned outside the village from which she was removed, orphic and orphaned, by her paternal family. Great Village and Boston/Worcester were her places of familial kinship/breaking (no plethora of relatives could replace a mother) cut by asthma and the insufficiencies of asthma medication in the 20th century.

Where a moose in bus headlights on a dark highway north of Parrsboro is the isthmus of breath itself. "a dim smell of moose, an acrid / smell of gasoline."

In poems, Bishop didn't (as did Rukeyser) "make something of experience"; she constructed "surprises" that seemed "natural." Not loquacious. When you can't breathe, there's no loquacity. You must hold back energy, to minimize the need for oxygen in the membranes. Bishop's poetry does this: holds back just one connection, just as she held back over half her poems, in the end, from publication, as 'unfinished.'

Bishop mixed real (eye) and synthetic (glass) to produce effects of disturbed surprise in the reader. But who *IS* this reader?

Though she wrote at times in voices or accents, Bishop saw her readers as being little different from herself in race and class. Her poems did not admit openly to economic or race privilege. I am sure she *realized* it, and there are glints, but her public did not require this admission, it took its own privilege for granted. On top of it, for years she publicly lauded that she did not teach, without acknowledging the more precarious circumstances of American poets who did. She simply did, she said, "what poetry entailed," but oh it was her means that allowed her to assert this.

Conditions of reception kept her insistently as lesbian in "closets and closets and closets." Her relation with *The New Yorker*'s delight in her light ironies (smoothed for the upper classes), her tolerance of their repunctuating (she claimed a ditziness regarding punctuation): these allowed her a material life in Brazil that was far from modest—and that depended on the poverty of a racialized community. There was the sports car she could not drive, a new garage, restoration of a third home, travel with Lota in Europe when Brazilian exchange rates were abysmal, the possibility to bank US-earned funds in Brazil where interest rates were high (and she encouraged others to do this too).

If conventional in the ways she chose to fit in, B. did not, in her writing, stick with convention. Her punctuation was syncopation that broke rules. If she rhymed, it was out of an admiring curiosity about rhyme. "Rhyme," she wrote in her journal at the time of her mother's death, "is mystical." She wanted rhyme to be invisible. Too visible, it was panto-rhyme, which she did not always shun, employing it deftly in poems like "To the Admirable Miss Moore." Bishop explored particularized lexicons and sonic values, studied rhyme in provençal poetry and Mother Goose simultaneously. Her study merged in "Visits to St Elizabeths" about visiting Pound in the asylum that bore her first name: a *House That Jack Built* for the man who made provençal poetry known in English. Her mix of registers disturbed her mentor Moore more than once, but EB resisted. She would insist on an 'ugly' word as its very precision was a honed beauty: the word 'garbage' belonged in the poem.

Her insistence on precise image and on sound (alliteration) led her to this mix of registers when choosing lexicon. To my delight, she displayed a certain whimsy about the whole program, and liked limerick over haiku. To her, 'funny' was profound, and I nod at this.

Oh her love of Edward Lear and—yes—*Pollyanna*, the orphan beloved of asthmatic girls! There's always something to be glad of!

She hated poetry readings, speeches, interviews. Her voice is steady in the tapes in the Room: her cadence seems to voice the New Criticism of the 1950s that came to represent all of poetry: elongating vowels, rising and falling in their elongation, punctuating with softly held consonants. Yet she slipped the bounds of this criticism.

Disturbed surprise.

In part, hers was a prepared voicing, like prepared piano. *The New Yorker* could alter her punctuation but never the rhythmics of her spoken voice—in which any Nova Scotian lilt is quelled but there is an attention to cadence, honed by her listening, her knowing that cadence too generates resonance and meaning. And cadence needs breath.

When I read her poems aloud, my voice cuts long vowels back to size and I like the poems better. Their aural tensilities and descriptive pulls and movements enter me.

The way she had fun with poetry, with rhyme, with nonsense verses: sonorous dexterity!

Her books become touchstones
sweet artifice

in archipelago-arcade
alongside, today

Norma Cole's *Where Shadows Will*
which lies on top of and beside

Lydia Cabrera and Édouard
Glissant: *Trembling Thinking*

Chus Pato
Un libre favor, m-Talá, Secesión, Sonora

Aimé Fernand David Césaire
Cahier d'un retour au pays natal

In the 1960s, the 'Mistometer.' *Isoproterenol*, analogue of epinephrine or adrenaline. Its effects of palpitations, nausea and fatigue mean it is rarely used today to treat asthma though the product monograph still lists: "temporary relief of mild symptoms of intermittent asthma." Temporary, mild, intermittent? You must be joking. The sentence walks backward twice as fast as it walks ahead! And there was Tedral: theophylline, ephedrine and phenobarbital combined (pulled at last from the market in 1993). Adrenaline injections. Aminophylline suppositories for slower absorption to prevent CNS failure. The body can breathe again but oh the heart roars, you have to stay still … and just breathe at last. (and Bishop smoked, and had cats, though she was allergic …)

(Meticorten — *prednisone*)

To live with poorly medicated asthma in any class conditions is hard, for breathing precedes every other human condition. You can't be a lesbian before you can breathe, a woman before you can breathe. I call it 'allergiqueer,' foreign to and preceding all category, an unstable structure—

Though she lived south of an anti-Communist and gay-perilous 1950s America that insisted on commercial optimism, Bishop was dependent on it in Brazil for validation and income. Commentators have long highlighted Bishop's drinking (Antabuse, the hospital cures), and a few pinpointed American politics—McCarthyism—as causal. But no one linked her drinking to *asthma*—and, ah, the euphoria of alcohol really does dull the constraint on breathing. Drinking was part of the effort Bishop took to *hush* who she was, in an era when this hushing was intense and natural. *Though (from her letters) she didn't find McCarthy to be nefarious.*

Andrés Ajens, radical Chilean poet of ethics and ethos, first made me turn to Bishop twenty years ago in his poem entitled (in Spanish) "Short/Stor" that bears the obvious epigraphic signature: "E. Bis-."

A breath, curtail-
ed, to *one art*

A structure unstable, not lopsided but 7-sided, perhaps: that crooked letter 7, its singular Art

If Ajens could read Bishop, I too could …

7

Two Centuries and a Lifetime, In Case You Were Wondering

EM

1

Asthma!
In my neck of the woods,
we are famished.

Your fantastic tales
we can live without,
you with

that Person
moulded around you
In the 21st century

finally, she is able
to breathe ...

2

Propped on pillows
Listening to voices outside
and watching
late northern sun

cast beam or shadow

In the 20th century
a gift meant to satisfy
or distract from
did not

an empty Jewel box,
ballerina on top,
wound up
spins to a little

tinnisch song.

3

Hopelessly
thinking *her* eyes and fingers
every moment

that kind of
hopeless
hoping she'll call ...

eyeing a Telephone receiver
and already
in the ribs' inner lining

touching a membrane around the lungs
touching the caul of the
heart, our

own organ ...
Why is it this marvellous?

And where does the marvel recede to,
in a sky's lifetime, breath

or vagary/ies

but into trees, winds, grasses,
other
marvellous things?

In Bishop's Brazilian poem "Under the Window: Ouro Prêto," the only one not drinking from the town spring is the voice speaking. The water pipe is site of village assembly, a traffic jam polluted with oil; the voice marvels at persons and vehicles below her but is foreign to that space, reads it at distance, from a window above. I think of Galicia across the Atlantic, its language the root of Portuguese, and how every fount there has waters of recognized qualities that may be sweet or sharp but if you feel an intimacy there you are of that water, made of that water.

The people whom the voice heard below the house were of that water, but the voice that heard was distant, omniscient, lifting their voices up out of their bodies, overhead into the "vast emptiness" of the poem.

In Bishop's poem, there is also a butterfly, iridescent in the water as oil is, drowning. Is a butterfly that can't fly a reference to breathing? To drink of the waters is curative and restores to you the water to which you belong. Or you are lost, or nearly lost....

The voice that described the scene outside and below the window's frame emanated from a human figure whose back was facing a room inside a house. To whom was the narrator speaking? Her lover behind her? Was she in *Lilli*'s bedroom? The poem a scene of clandestine lesbian love?

Always already lesbian love is outside of the space and time of the polis, outside its waters. Lesbian love would be a futurity not destined to be revealed in Bishop's poem, yet always just on the brink of appearing.

Or was always in full sight, but 'not there.'

I too am of this water, this intimacy....

Bishop's relation to class difference: in "House Guest," wry in whimsy, the poet's voice came close to gentle self-mockery and self-awareness, but did it really illuminate the poem's subject, the seamstress? That depends on the conditions of reception, and my own condition as an immigrant's daughter is not ideal:

Read E. Bishop's "House Guest"
http://poemz.org/elizabeth-bishop/house-guest

I hear the narrator as being from a class outside and above the seamstress (perhaps, as in "Manuelzinho," it was her lover Lota's voice that EB imitated?); it is a voice wryly exasperated, wanting to pour money on the seamstress, and imagining her an inner life likely not the seamstress's at all. The poem almost disdains the possibility that working women think. I read the narrator as privileged, one who doesn't live the complexities of Brazil as an ordinary citizen—she can always, at any moment, opt to leave, or spend. Spending is the solace she sees for the seamstress. Though Gillian White says of Bishop that she "was thinking through a formidable ethical discourse about forms of attention and writing, and the subject position they implied," I am not sure. Maybe for readers of *The New Yorker* of 7 December 1968, "House Guest" was a look into another world, but if you come from my world ... not so much.

Bishop's migration to Brazil was that of tourist-exile. A tourist is always foreign to a public, makes no claim to reporting. A lesbian in that time existed under similar conditions. Even today, in a world more open to gender and sexual difference, a lesbian can feel a tourist in the world painted by most people around her.

Asthma is more primary: to be an allergic person is to be foreign to all persons. Here, the technical brilliance, taut whimsy, reticence of Bishop takes on more sense. Born 40 years later, she'd have *had* more freedom to not silence her desires, and to think of conditions of production and reception when writing of those outside her own race and class. And meds would have improved. She would have been, like me as I write this, medicated but able to breathe.

(Later I read that the house guest was "sister of one of L.'s aristocratic friends"—not a travelling seamstress at all. Oh readerly reception, oh reversal!)

In Galician and Portuguese (*in Canada too, my mother's friend the Irish dressmaker, single mother*) traditional economies, women did go from house to house, village to village, to sew. Seamstress/spinner held key histories of women's lives and community. Piecework economy involved women's labour—laundress, housekeeper, seamstress—and men's—knife-sharpening, umbrella repair, cooking pot and roof/wall repair, rag recuperation. Sewing is a profession of service, of financial precarity, working inside the house, unlike the male repairers, yet not really a 'house guest' *(my mother deliberately never learned when young to sew or embroider well, and made sure I didn't—though she revered the 'dressmaker' and later took courses, regretting her youthful defiance).*

Galician poet Uxío Novoneyra, child in the 1930s, asthmatic thus often confined to home, recalled the spinner in his mountain home. In a short poem, he turned his suppositions about her around: *two* minds were moving, one of them his:

—SPINNING girl so lissome
always aspinning
aspinning and dreaming
with nothing to show.
—With nothing to show
oh that's still to be seen
as with the fibres of linen
in twisting them lean
something's bound to get caught.
—Something's bound to get caught
and good faith you are right
for I've had my eye on you
not realizing quite—
I've been caught up with falling in love.

Bishop's "House Guest" is sly, lighthearted, deprecatory not sweet. Her seamstress is silent; the words put in her mouth attend instead to the poet who controls the poem's "flick of impudence." Perhaps the seamstress is a trope for Bishop herself, dissatisfied with what she sews (poems)? Novoneyra returns in his poem to himself, asthmatic boy watching the spinner for hours. In his case, the spinner is the outside world of wonder, and he is falling in love with this world—this silent world—with *nothing to show*. Or with *something* … love.

In the 1970s, asthma medications still contained barbiturates. They sped you up to slow you down, and led to confusions, stupors. Bishop also took Dexamyl (amphetamine) and Nardil (monoamine oxidase inhibitor) as a "booster" (i.e. antidepressant), cortisone for asthma, Anorexyl (appetite suppressant to control weight gain from cortisone), Antabuse (to inhibit alcohol consumption), Premarin for menopause. A pharmacopœia of chemicals by which …

… patriarchal society and Capital did and do control women's bodies (by controlling bodily or psychic states known as 'ailments')—even bodies whom it does not otherwise control via financial precarity. (Men too it controls, yes, more with opiate derivatives for pain.) None of us lives outside Capital, and a poetics that just hints at but does not pursue politico-economic reflection remains transcendent, incapable of effecting or imagining change. Incapable of uprooting its own optic.

Imagine, instead, a layered commonality, an ecology of thresholds. Seven-sidedness as ecology, not as unstable form. A threshold can exist as well in a vertical field (not just horizontal). South to north.

That Bishop found the tourist eye suspect in "Questions of Travel" is apt to these equations. She did not reveal how she sensed the conditions of her own reception but was aware, in this poem at least, of the privileged lie inherent in the conditions of her own speaking:

"Should we even be here? Shouldn't we stay home?"

Staying home in the Covid-19 pandemic. Shut in. The law says I can see no one. When I search the internet for 'dressing gown white with red cats,' this image of a cat dressed as a nurse keeps reappearing.

It has nothing to do with my dressing gown but it startles and dismays me. For *what* is it an avatar? For what conjunction of unnamed feelings?

What does it have to do with poetry?

Something in it insists at me

When I search instead, not daring to hope, for 'white fabric with stylized red cats,' I get hundreds of images of fabric face masks for sale. Few or none of them have to do with cats. The word 'fabric' is now dehistoricized by the pandemic around me.

Hello Covid.

Reading EB's Letters Written During the War and Holocaust 1939–1945

Elisa Sampedrín, for EM

Before the light
was torn from us

piecemeal, in strips
lights dismaying us

before we could be
born

a war on this near
horizon

roosters, tissue-paper
peonies, broccoli

alphabets are never
in disgrace

yet a homeopathy lies
in every letter

She wrote from New York
on her way south to the shabby glitter and gals of
Key West

Oh Elizabeth oh, *Zaza, Betchy, Bishie, Bysshe, Cookie, Bis-*
Why not ever a word from you in letters

all war long
of *war?**

**she did note that the expansion of the Navy base was ruining her Key West neighbourhood, and she couldn't get to Europe to vacation …*

The New Yorker only took poems of its 'type,' serious with a flick of knowing whimsy, no homosexual hints: Bishop abetted more than she rebelled. At her first teaching gig (detaching herself from Brazilian life and suspending her *New Yorker* contract) in 1966 in Seattle, it was her 'non-teaching' that intrigued interviewers—only able to interview her *because* she was there to teach. "Perhaps her absence from the campus, the clique and the cocktail circuit is partly responsible for the freshness and originality of her work," offered Tom Robbins in *Seattle* that year.

The campus is a place of *labour* for many, where some via ideas move knowledge forward, so a place of hope—but also of abuses of labour. Yet Robbins alliterates campus with clique and cocktail circuit—knowing that sound produces meaning: a slick upper-class view.

For some writers, not-teaching can seem to shut them out of a literary validation they crave. Bishop seemed to deride them. Yet she already had validation and *was* Establishment: Vassar, Pulitzer, Library of Congress, Harvard, two Guggenheims, Neustadt. Embraced yet outside at once.

A decade post-Seattle, in Rotterdam, Bishop said she'd not been to Brazil for two years, adding "I had friends living there, but they'd died. I still have a house there and it still has to be sold." How she pluralized the death of her beloved Lota (her 'they' is no g-neutral pronoun here) and made a fast switch to real estate, segueing from her house in Ouro Prêto to a prestige Boston condominium by the harbour, where she'd rather be. "But first," she confided, "I have to go to Lisbon to see friends. And to swim." *J. Bernlef, 1976*

Houses were for public consumption, her lover not. It was the 1970s, still a perilous time to admit homosexual relationships though less perilous than during the Cold War. Bishop admired the "sexual courage" of Auden but felt it was not hers to assume. That the personal was no one's business was a matter of safety. To expose the personal was a trust violation (she gently accused Lowell of this when he used his ex-wife's letters in *The Dolphin*, 1972).

Her personal is not my business either. Time's threshold is changed; I see from a perspective not open to B. "The past is a foreign country; they do things differently there." (L. P. Hartley, *The Go-Between*, 1953)

Later, teaching at Harvard, renting then settled (after difficulties manoeuvring her inheritance from Lota past currency controls and out of Brazil) into her wharfside condominium, she aimed to teach long enough to qualify for 'medical benefits' when she retired—"extremely important," she wrote to her retired *New Yorker* editor in January '76 (often hospitalized, she knew the costs of care were unaffordable otherwise). She was wrong about the retirement benefits, and taught semesters at various universities till the end of her life.

She taught so as^{thma} to *breathe.*

Bishopric

EM

Yet what poet wouldn't
give their worn eye-teeth to have written
even her unpublished poems!

She's more personable there, more
wondering, unstable, thrilled by mistakes
of diction,
humorous (evoking Edward Lear—whose
poems she's avid for)
even, in love with girls and dreaming,
there are beds, many beds, in hotels and homes
everywhere beds
where the travelling (of the bourgeois woman) descends
happily to sheet-level,
and there's the carpet smell

and gay-iety.

In deft intercalation of registers, metres, subjects and perspectives, EB made space-time shift in fractals that seem smooth but perturb. Just slightly. Was restraint *modern*? (registers and juxtapositions, but no syntactic imbroligos) Her poems did disrupt narrative closure and coherence (implicating the observer in the slant triangle of description) to achieve effects that Lowell (1970) called her "*luminism (meaning radiance and compression, etc).*" (vague discomfit)

In a letter to poet May Swensen, Bishop: "… my point about 'physical' words is hard to explain … It's a problem of placement, choice of word, abruptness or accuracy of the image—and does it help or detract?"

In the deflective exactitude she strove for, even the abrupt word had to *help*, not detract. She had a spatial sense of sound, and of sound affect.

I have never wished for honed beauty in the poem so as "to give an esthetic experience," as EB wrote in that same letter, but "methodic obliqueness" works. A certain *taut unravelling* in diction, which in medieval times in Iberia among the wanderers (*os vagaceiros*) indicated mastery of form: not how well you can follow form, or yes that, but how well the poet can make it shift just slightly, awakening a sensation in the throat of the listener.

Bishop is, then, medieval. A praise-

(is the dog beautiful?
limping in front of the drugstore)

Further in this letter of 3 July 1958, EB writes of 'experience' in response to something MS raised, possibly meaning lived experience, *as 'writing from one's experience' was in the American air. The very idea made EB balk: "… there is no way of telling what really is 'experience' anyway, it seems to me. Look at what Miss Moore has done with what would seem to me to be almost none …"*

She also refused to be classed as a 'woman poet' in anthologies, and struggled against editors, men and women, who felt women should write about smaller domestic things. Not fishhouses. Perhaps no one should write about fishhouses …

deflected curbside
sentiment as a kind of metrical continuity
metre's deflection an impeded resonance
(paradox)
(more resonant)
the appearance of a regularity
noted via an interrupted pattern

the mind is not at rest
naturally

Again, who is her reader?
(obuses landing in a caustic cloud)

Who is mine? Mine is perhaps: my mother, who didn't read poetry. The nurse who came home tired (without her profession, how would I have survived?). And, always, persons unknown to me (hello!) who struggle, for whom financial dailiness is not a given, control of anxiety is not a given, joy is present but fleeting, the grasses, the social order and its safety are not a given: queer practice in my time, lesbian practice acknowledges its links to all these other precarities, whereas in Bishop's time, her queer practice was a vanishing

up up into the vast vast emptiness

with chinks or gaps, though, entries/exits
in the poems themselves ...

~~lyric's arbiter tracks in scabrous shoes~~ 7

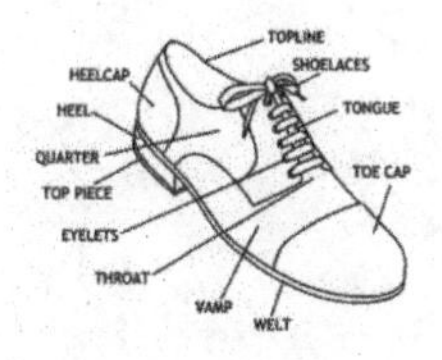

Gas Station

EM, in imitation

Oh, the smell of oil!
—this little gas station,
dirt-ingrained, oil-soaked
to a wondrous infinite
black translucency.
Just don't light a cig!

Father wears oil-primed
workwear coveralls
gone tight in the armpits,
and a gaggle of quick flirty
grease-monkey sons help
(it's a family business),
workworn, hand-wiping,
polite.

The station is their front yard!
From their cement porch they
can watch the pumps, from
sun-faded patio furniture;
on the wicker chair
the family pup lords it over all.

There are comics
and old mags too—a flash
of bright colour—on the cloth
over the table beside
a robust fur-leafed begonia.

It's a home to be proud of
in the age of gasoline!
Gas, diesel, mufflers,
change your winter tires
check the transmission,
reset the tappet timing.

And in between customers,
sit out on the front porch—
watch cars zoom past the pumps
from beside the begonia.

Someone keeps it neat around
here too, someone hidden
waters plants. Someone
steps down to arrange the shelves of
motor oil so the labels sing out
to passing vehicles.
This one—our hidden someone—
(ESSEnce or ESSO)
perhaps never dreamed this
would become her life.

In Altadore, the White Rose down my street became Royalite in the early '60s, then BA when BA bought Royalite, then Stevo Auto Clinic in 1969 till now. Owned by our neighbour Johnny Rand when it was White Rose and Royalite, it had two bays, one with pit and one with hoist, surrounded by tools and bolts. We were kept out and would sit in the office instead, unwilling to leave, smelling the oil and reading magazines laid out for those awaiting repairs (a little library). How I loved the station, and its strings of coloured flags over the gas pumps snapping wildly in the prairie hot wind … Being *and* driving *were the same to us … ESSE (m.), ESSA (f.) and ISSO (n.) is 'that' in Portuguese. ESSO seems to combine them. ESSE in Latin is 'to be.'*

Comeuppance

Elisa Sampedrín

I am not used to what is sluggish
or forgotten

Temperament or indolence
oh indolence

My vase of glass
Her artful

smile across a table lit by only
one sunset

Ha ha
You don't deserve me

Artful or sluggish or
forgotten

Oh forgotten indolence
comeuppance you are

esso, isso, este, isto: A zeal

The desire that utterances exist in a language other than that in which they are created: translation. In the body, an awareness of where in the mouth a particular language is spoken. Between languages, form is not still.

"From the audience," R. told me, "I saw your mouth change. I saw how your left leg moved, as axis." Translation is a way of bringing poetry into intimate ions, one's own body. It's the most intimate relationship with a poem that there is. A leg to lean on, not a zeal.

Bishop's conditions of production for 16 years included proximity of Brazilian Portuguese; its sounds and mouth entered her. At Vassar, she'd translated French, Spanish, Portuguese, Greek and Latin: a classical education. In her 16 Brazil years, she translated but 12 poems, co-edited an anthology of Brazilian poetry in translation, scripted the *Life* coffee-table book *Brazil* that to her chagrin was edited so as to portray *their* bland cheer to US investors (her own politics at the time were problematic, but more aware), translated stories by Leme neighbour Clarice Lispector and the diary of Helena, white girl in a mining town whose name was a pseudonym and book heavily edited by her spouse. To Bishop, it was: "a real diary, told by a real girl."

EB's conditions of production included making 'truth' of something that had seeds in truth but was constructed, and not outwardly admitting the construct. While struggling against the constructs of others.

Outside her own culture, in Brazil, Bishop was able to write of Nova Scotia, the Fundy shore, her village childhood. In many ways, she seemed to set herself *outside* Portuguese; she read its literature but did not cultivate literary contacts or renown. She remained insistently American. She mimed Brazilian pronunciation, for example of 'Elizabeth' as 'Elizabetchy,' without admitting this pronunciation is normal speech, presenting Portuguese to her English readers as a defective/deflective version of their own (supposedly neutral) tongue.

Art was her country. *How to say the felt thing? Is breath felt? Silence?*

How to say the felt thing in its directness, un(h)armed by diction's decoration?

Bishop didn't like social verse: hers was a belief in the twist and surprise of language, image, diction. But she asserted that the social *could* be carried in *popular* form. Her 1964 poem "The Burglar of Babylon" echoed Brazilian samba forms and *literatura de cordel* (poems often on social issues printed cheaply, with woodcuts, hung from strings in markets, performed at times, to lure buyers). After it appeared in *The New Yorker*, the poem masqueraded four years later as a children's book with woodcuts called *The Ballad of…*, confusing critics in its new incarnation. As reviewed by *Kirkus*: "The idea is interesting, the audience is doubtful, the material is dubious." And *Goodreads*: "This seems like a children's book but you can't imagine reading it to a child."

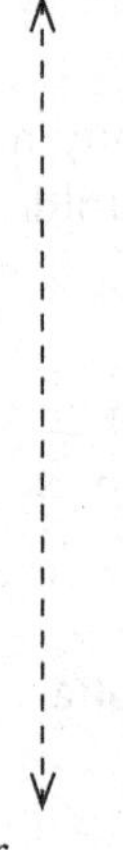

from an EB letter to Anne Stevenson, 8 January 1964:

"My outlook is pessimistic. I think we are still barbarians, barbarians who commit a hundred indecencies and cruelties every day of our lives, as just possibly future ages may be able to see. But I think we should be gay in spite of it, sometimes even giddy, – to make life endurable and to keep ourselves 'new, tender, quick.'"

With *literatura de cordel* and samba as models, EB had scripted the last hours of Milton Santos de Almeida, *Micuçú*, 28-year-old fugitive and *marginal* hunted by a force of 1,000 police on 19 January 1964 in the *mata* atop Chapéu Mangueira, a *favela* on the *morro* of Babylon, while the rich below in Leme watched with binoculars. Bullet-shattered, marched bleeding from the *morro* to a police jeep, Micuçú was put paid by a police bullet behind the ear.

There is something contrary about the way that Bishop found to 'highlight inequities in Brazil,' as some said, yet portraying the poor as fearful, and as lichen. In Rio, the rich can't look "down" on the poor; they must look uphill. No poor person, though, would (as the poem does) call their house a "stain," let alone see their community as "fearful"—perhaps it was the papers calling Micuçú *temível bandido*, fearsome bandit, that drew Bishop to that word. Bishop wrote nothing that would upset those of Leme or *The New Yorker*. Their values, which she'd assumed, condition the work. *Though she does admit Micuçú was shot while running away, not confronting the police.*

Bishop claimed *micuçu* was "Indian" for snake, or could be short for *mico*, marmoset monkey. But *mico* is also a gaffe, a faux pas, a *papelão*. His name could simply be 'l'il gaffer,' playing with the M of his first name (and name of a blind English poet). Or the poem itself could be a kind of gaffe, a *mico*, a way to *facer mico*, downfall, *cadoiro* …

Or a paraded song of samba …

A will … to breathe …

The breath of words, wording outward in the samba-read-as-ballad, was charged with Bishop's ideological markers, those that condition reception: *the vast vast emptiness …*

Samba rhythms arose in Black communities in and around Rio de Janeiro early in the 20th century, era of migration from drought-ridden NE sugar fields to coffee plantations of the SE. They were persecuted until Vargas in 1935 appropriated samba as part of the nationalism of his quasi-fascist Estado Novo, and funded the Escolas where teams vie each year to write the winning Carnaval song. As popular verse, samba kept its ties to the underclasses, its echoes of Yoruba culture. As in bardic song, samba found ways to speak griefs and humours that could be held in the socius and not stopped by the authorities. Vargas's embrace was economic: eyeing tourism dollars.

In the north, we think of Carnaval as do tourists: as parade and costumed dancers. But *samba-enredo* lyric is key. It rings out the news—as do bardic songs of all times and cultures—from the viewpoint of the downtrodden, in ways that slip past censure. (Oft-times the bard, historically, is blind. The Ukrainian *kobzar*, the hurdy-gurdy-playing wanderer in Rosalía de Castro. Milton. Words are breath not eyes. *Glass eye.*)

Bishop translated Micuçú via rhythms and norms of samba, borrowed from the matted *morros* of Rio and their *favelas* of rough homes without water, sewers, electric light, perched on winding paths in the *mata*, jungle, above her society home. Though entranced by samba, she didn't publicly acknowledge it but called her poem English ballad, in a register she denominated "fausse naïve." But it was fausse *samba*. "Fausse" because real samba is *wise*, breathes memory of forced ocean crossings, slavery and migration, forced silence that resists, is defiant not naive!

The word *favela* came from the name of a tree in the NE whose leaves sting the skin it touches—just as the makeshift tiny homes spilling down the *morros* of Rio stung the eyes of its middle and upper classes …

Above Leme and Copacabana, the *Babilônia* favela held folk come south to build the army fort and allied with the military dictatorship. *Chapéu Mangueira* (named after a hat factory) was beside it, home to builders and domestics recently migrated from the interior who fought military dictatorship and the constant threat of demolition; its associations were communist and built public works that today still offer care. This is where Micuçú was caught.

Perhaps the name 'Babylon' was more euro-poetic to Bishop as a title, more comfortable to her as a resident of moneyed Leme …

Santos de Almeida did not live in *Babilônia*, though his aunt did. His was favela *São Carlos*, near his mom in *Catumbí*. The papers reported that he loved his two children, who lived with their maternal grandma as their mom had remarried. He gave all children money, was a shoemaker, beloved by all. His life of crime started at 12 when he bought a stolen radio; it was only after a jail term that he became an outlaw.

In Bishop's poem, though she could read news in Portuguese, Micuçú was a murderer, an "enemy of society" and "mean" even as a baby. Not, as he was to his family: *new, tender, quick.*

> *Wherefore be cheer'd, and praise him to the full*
> *Each day, each houre, each moment of the week,*
> *Who fain would have you be new, tender, quick.*

That's George Herbert, a Bishop favourite poem called "Love Unknown."

In her poem, Bishop abstracted her voice, that of a spectator amid the rich-with-binoculars (in letters she admitted: *I was one of them*), and triangulated the story: as the narrator detaches from the specularity of the binocular-holders, she shifts closer to Micuçú, the gaffe. But never arrives at him, or hears him out. He's dead.

A scant three months after this police chase/murder in the favela, on 31 March 1964 (a decade after the suicide of Vargas, a "minor dictator"), a military coup led by "a few brave generals" (B.'s words) brought a dictatorship that lasted 21 years.

The blind poet, the poet as blind, the poet who gazes via the glass eye of binoculars, claiming blind to see, ahead, the kites of heaven, kobzar, кобзар

And the perfection of a sunset and dog tracks in sand

The vulva (in Guatemalan Spanish, mico could be 'cunt')

How to say the felt thing? The emotion of off-rhyme, the sting-stain, the man laid out, one ear to the ground, mouth up and open, visible in the papers, the gaffe

Severed in time and space from its samba and *cordel* impulses and base, Bishop's ballad was published on 13 November 1964 (speedy, for EB) in *The New Yorker*, on two facing pages, with the remaining space holding a large cartoon of

a corporate boardroom.

What chance did Micuçú have?

He was slain twice.

To the eternity of her text, samba yet adheres as temporal movement of lingual resistance. Translation is resistant form. Though Bishop claimed to work from English ballad as if for children (easier to present in America), shrouding samba, the poem resists her appropriation (and reviewers were skeptical). All translations do this, resist a new temporal threshold or interface that might conceal their difference. Bishop cannot make her poem out to be "fausse naïve."

Translations age and need redoing (as they are readings, and readings are always contemporary), whereas texts, on aging, simply gather exegesis. Exegesis is reverence, points to the eternal. Translation is a cut in time, and its texts bleed time and are often later discarded, bled out. Its perpetuity falls away. It is not naive. Black Brazilian culture born of forbidden speech has today long outlived Bishop's *gaffe*.

Responsibility—attunement—ethics. Remembering a talk on translation and ethics I once wrote for a keynote speech that, once I'd arrived, I was not welcome to give. *sintaxualité, sintextualidade, sintexualité …*

If this book you now hold (si ce livre) is a translator's entry (est l'intrusion d'une traductrice) as foreigner (coma forasteira) into the work and breath (dans les œuvres et le souffle) of three modernist American women poets (de trois poètes américaines modernistes): what ethics here? (qui sait, quen se sabe?)

"It's heart-f***ing-breaking," Iris Turcott (15 January 2013) said to me on the telephone of *Kapusta*, an unproduceable play. A deafening foreign-ation.

Did you say something? ~~It was not recorded.~~ Oh L'il Gaffer. I didn't hear.

A poem (like silence) listen?
(this whole book, it occurs to me suddenly, is refusal, is an attempt at the *something else* … a *listening-sorrow forward hear*)

The marvel of Bishop's temporal movements into English, for there is marvel too: how she translated poems from Portuguese that seemed at times to speak of her own life. If she couldn't speak of it directly, translations could.

Archaic Torso of ~~Apollo~~ Asthma

Elisa Sampredrín, gaffed from Rilke (argh Elisa, why?)

We cannot know this legendary dressing gown
with cats like red fruit. And yet its torso
is so suffused with wheezing from inside,
like a lamp, in which the gaze turns low
and it gleams in all its power. Otherwise
the curved breastbone of the asthmatic girl
could not dazzle us so, nor could
a smile run through the placid hips and thighs
to that navel where a mother once held her fast.
It's not that this memory would seem defaced
beneath the translucent cascade of the shoulders,
it's that, unseen in dark, its stutter is erased
and cannot, from the stitched borders of its red piping,
burst like a star: for here there is no place
that sees her. She's you. Yes, you, breathing.
Fatalist, you must get dressed.

Poema de Sete Faces

Carlos Drummond de Andrade

Quando nasci, um anjo torto
Desses que vivem na sombra
Disse: Vai, Carlos! Ser *gauche* na vida.

As casas espiam os homens
Que correm atrás de mulheres.
A tarde talvez fosse azul,
Não houvesse tantos desejos.

O bonde passa cheio de pernas:
Pernas brancas pretas amarelas.
Para que tanta perna, meu Deus, pergunta meu coração.
Porém meus olhos
Não perguntam nada.

O homem atrás do bigode
É sério, simples e forte.
Quase não conversa.
Tem poucos, raros amigos
O homem atrás dos óculos e do bigode.

Meu Deus, por que me abandonaste
Se sabias que eu não era Deus,
Se sabias que eu era fraco.

Mundo mundo vasto mundo,
Se eu me chamasse Raimundo
Seria uma rima, não seria uma solução.
Mundo mundo vasto mundo,
Mais vasto é meu coração.

Eu não devia te dizer
Mas essa lua
Mas esse conhaque
Botam a gente comovido como o diabo.

7-Sided Poem*

~~*Carlos*~~ *Drummond de Andrade, trans-altered by ES (Bishop translated it too)*

When I was born, a crooked angel
One of those who live in shadow
Said: Go, Bishie! Be *gauche* in life!

Houses watch the gals
Who chase after women
If afternoon were blue
Desires might've been fewer

The tram passes full of legs
Legs white black yellow
Why so many legs, my god, my heart asks
While my eyes
Are glass

The gal sans moustache
Is serious, simple, strong
Often too shy to speak
Has friends few, rare
The gal behind the glasses, sans moustache

My god why hast thou forsaken me
Knowing I was ungodly
Knowing I was frail

World world vast world
If I were named Pearl
It would rhyme, but what's that solve.
World world vast world
Vaster is my heart's evolve.

I shouldn't say this
But this moon
But this *Pitú cachaça*
Stir up the devil in a gal.

*A 7-sided structure is by nature unstable. This is a lesbo drinking poem. Bishop can't be so forthright in her own poems, but in a translation ... yes!

In her last home, on Boston's newly gentrified Lewis Wharf, Bishop created a simulacrum of Brazilian homes she'd lost, a lair or *lar* of art and folk objects, statuettes of saints whose robes she changed in keeping with saints' days and celebrations, looking out on the sea or spring. Her tables were Brazilian. Her shelves held works of Brazilian literature in Portuguese.

Alongside Edward Lear. And *Pollyanna*. Works asthmatics cling to. As if rhyme helps breathing, and those short of breath deal with misfortune by being irrepressibly glad. In a "flick of impudence," Elizabeth Bishop claimed her first rhyme was *gasoline/Vaseline*. Her grandmother'd used a bit of each to polish white/black saddle shoes, one for each colour.

From letters to her doctor, I extract an Elizabethan Pollyannic litany:

Everything is fine
Apart from that, everything is fine
Everything is fine, except
I have no right to bother you as everything is fine

I just can't breathe.
I just can't sleep at night or lie down flat.
I just hope that if I don't move it will go away.
I cough and choke.

Everything is fine.
Everything is fine

(She dedicated *Cold Spring* to her doctor, Anny Bermann. In French, the cold spring sounds even colder: *Printemps froid*. 1955. The year I breathed my first breaths.)

Yet, in other letters, the pleas for breath, for breathing:

Breathing

I'm so full of ***adrenaline, morphine,*** *and a particularly drugged and poisonous kind of cough syrup (lightheaded, 1935) : Having asthma steadily for several weeks, taking about 2 cc of* ***adrenaline*** *every night (Cape Breton, July 1947) :* ***2 cc during the day and 3 or 4 during the night;*** *I stayed in bed yesterday thinking if I didn't move it might help (CB 1947) :* ***Along with the asthma a rash*** *on my wrist and arm : Is there something drastic you can* ***prescribe me*** *The* ***nebulizers*** *never seemed to do any good after the asthma really gets going (July 1947) : The Cape Breton doctor drove over the mtns one night, left me a supply of* ***adrenaline and ephedrine and ephedrine capsules*** *(make me nauseated and dizzy, still taking injections 2 or 3 times a day and 3 or 4 times during the night) :* ***I really don't know what to do*** *There is so much I want to do here &* ***I can scarcely get up & down stairs*** *:* ***Hundreds of little blisters*** *(Benadryl worked to clear it up) : Except for the asthma almost everything is fine (December 1947) : Everything is fine except that I am getting* ***awfully tired of constantly having asthma*** *(December 1947) : I ran out of* ***theoglycinate*** *so I have had to use* ***adrenline,*** *3 cc in the course of every evening and night and I am constantly coughing, choking :* ***For the last 8 or 9 years I have had asthma almost every day and night.*** *I've never been able to lie down in bed, etc., and I am getting very tired of it ... (1947) : But I have asthma every night and even with the* ***theoglycinate pills*** *I have to take one or two shots of* ***adrenaline*** *in the night (1948 Key West)—(at least in the daytime I seem to have enough wind for swimming) : I am having asthma constantly, usually clearing up in the morning and then beginning again around 4pm; pretty bad because one night I ran out of the* ***sulfate cartridges*** *and had to take* ***four shots of adrenaline.*** *(1950)*

EM: I don't care what ~~Helen Vendler~~ has to say about her poetry.

I only want to breathe.

Nothing about the pandemic terrifies me except that pharmacies might run out of my meds and I would not be able to breathe. My friends, too, scare me. At times they assume illnesses they don't have when it's expedient (a special plate in a restaurant, a vaccine appointment). They have no clue.

No one knows me. (abet is time's inter/face)

(My mother, long dead, knows me.)

signed,

Abraços e saudades
-E.

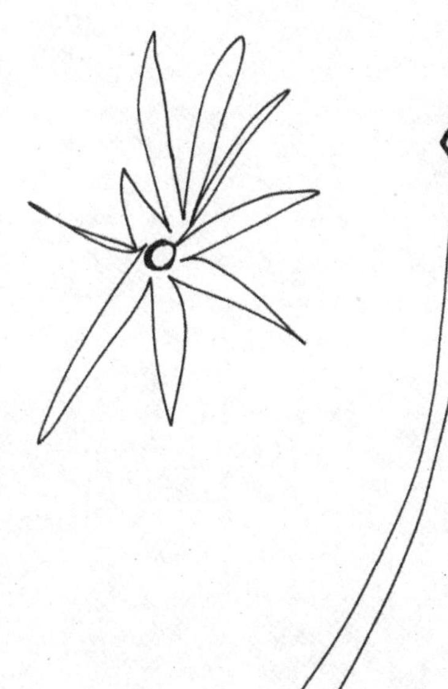

AWG

Boston, MA, 1880–New York City, 1958

Beware, Beware, O Land o' Dreams
The black giant sleeps unquiet yet awhile;
Anon, he turns to ease his tired side.
Beware, O Land o' Dreams!

from an early poem, uncollected

To the north, the victorious rebels did not extend their revolutionary principles to include the unfree, and by 1787 it was clear that the new nation would be built in large measure on the backs of the enslaved black workers who constituted fully a fifth of the population of the United States.

Julius S. Scott, *The Common Wind*

The *fenda* is a real place too.

E.S. "Solitud

Islant: the 'is' of *silent* is backwards, is I-slant

The Room's archive of American voices is silent to Angelina Weld Grimké. I did not hear her. No recording of her voicing is held on Earth let alone in the Woodberry. Her breath is not archived. Yet silent will not mean absent, not mean non-breath. What a Room contains is constituted by what is Outside it. The grammar of 'silent' demands *is. AWG is* the poet whose truth will not accrue to the general relation that is 'America' no matter what she will enact or say, because 'Black' means she could not *act* or *speak* as a being *among equals*

Silence will be the socius's response to her voice and language (Arendt's *Human Condition* leaves her out), and this still adheres

The imprints of her words will be … engrams …
Her breath will be futures …

(Glissant's 'opacity'—
that difference should not oblige Transparency:
"this-here is the weave and it weaves no boundaries")

« Elles [les questions de la traduction catachrestique, postcoloniale de la modernité] nous obligent à introduire la question de l'agent subalterne dans la question de la modernité : quel est ce 'maintenant' de la modernité ? Qui définit ce présent d'où nous parlons ? Ce qui nous amène à une question plus problématique encore : *quel est le désir de cette demande répétée de modernisation ?* » Homi Bhabha, *Les lieux de la culture* tr. Françoise Bouillot (traductrice d'Agatha Christie entre autres …)

"These are the issues of the catachrestic, postcolonial translation of modernity. They force us to introduce the question of subaltern agency, into the question of modernity: what is this 'now' of modernity? Who defines this present from which we speak? This leads to a more challenging question: *what is the desire of this repeated demand to modernize?*"
Homi Bhabha, *The Location of Culture*

'Angelina Weld Grimké will migrate into silence' is a mark of white archival silence, i.e. my voice, not hers

A reading of AWG's works and grasp of her conditions of production show why my speech fails//

Acutely aware of these conditions of reception
she will choose to do something 'else'

Here the archive crumbles et qu'est-ce qu'on pourrait faire ?

« Un jour, Amérique, je vous tournerai le dos »*

the archipelago
AWG's migration/real&Imagined

Boston Washington Charleston New York Santo Domingo

the archipelago
AWG's migration

… where is *Angelina*? Certainly not in these laconic notes that register their presence in the archive…. nor are they outside the archive, in a biographical reality of which we know literally nothing. They stand on the threshold of the text in which they are put into play, or, rather, their absence, their eternal turning away, is marked on the outer edge of the archive, like the gesture that has both rendered it possible and exceeded and nullified its intention.

Profanations, Giorgio Agamben, tr. Jeff Fort,
one word altered

In Grimké's 1916 play *Rachel*, the young protagonist—ravaged by segregation's grip and news images of lynched Black bodies—refuses fecundity, decides not to bring children into a world where racism will harm them. Grimké's Rachel simply refuses to be matriarch, instead exercises the freedom to choose a future via one's own female body. It is her *act*. Rachel's unborn children (to whom she speaks in the play), Brian Russell Roberts suggests, are "metonymies of

absent speech."

This first play by an African-American woman to be produced in mainstream theatre will refuse, too, to re-enact the minstrel-show aesthetic that dogged white-driven cultural stagings and obscured Black life.

Time in the play passes via European paintings on a wall: opening with Millet's *The Reaper* (Grimké says *reapers*, and yes, two figures appear): a man, seen from the back, is scything. Race indeterminate, muscles taut under his shirt, he brings in the fruit of the land. In Act II, four years later, this painting is gone, replaced by Millet's *The Man with the Hoe*: a man exhausted, lips wind-split, faces the viewer, hoeing barren ground.

He could be Black. There will be no harvest.

The *natality* of Hannah Arendt, the *nationelle* of Hölderlin—that to which we are born—is a freedom that is 'gratuit,' freely granted/gifted. *Un libre favor*, as in Chus Pato, echoing Kant.

In *The Human Condition* (1958)
Hannah Arendt ties 'action' to natality,
to human birth as 'miracle' of new life
and thus new possibility for speech and action.

Grimké in America will involute this European view long before Arendt will write it. In her experience as Black woman reading Southern US news of lynchings, and out of the *a-natality* of brutally hung (male) figures, Grimké in *Rachel* will project *a-fecundity*, posit refusal not as absence of action but as its involution, which makes it an action still and puts it in front of us, to come.

Her anachronism vis-à-vis Arendt (who wrote later) is truly *archipelago* as "passage to the crossroads of the world" (José Martí)

American critics will assail Grimké for wishing decimation of her race. Yet G. wills not the extinction of her race but shows that at the core of natality/action lies a twist of silence/silencing/hanging fire. In her life she will enact this twist and 'cease writing,' they will say, or will—by a-writing—enact with her body a performative elocution of silence as a freeing mechanism from the constraints of Black life in her time. To struggle against the racist founding of America itself, a *vita activa* will demand this 'involuted choice.'

in·vo·lu·tion /ˌinvəˈlo͞oSHən/
noun
2. MATHEMATICS
   a function, transformation, or operator that is equal to its inverse, i.e. which gives the identity when applied to itself.
1. PHYSIOLOGY
   the shrinkage of an organ in old age or when inactive, e.g. of the uterus after childbirth.

Outward

Elisa Sampedrín

I was given a bit of hardship
and my face ran from it

I was given a bit of hardship
and my face just ran

First it ran forward out of the *hütte*
in its consternation

Its confusion was the homelessness
of its desire

So my face ran forward and hopeful
of somewhere

It was always in front of me hoping
facing outward

not facing me but facing air's mishap
facing out to your face

facing outward
as I ran

Grimké's father Archibald—lawyer, US diplomat, civil rights activist; his own father, Henry, a white planter-enslaver and his mother, Nancy Weston, Henry's nurse and slave—went North to Lincoln University with his brother Francis after the Civil War freed them (upon H.'s death, they, their brother John, and mother were left as chattel to a white half-brother who was to free them and did not), where, upon graduation—covered in the press—they were seen and welcomed as nephews by two Boston aunts, sisters of Henry. They will continue their education at Harvard and Princeton, in law and theology.

Angelina, Archie's daughter, will be an only child; her mother, turned Unitarian on marrying Archie, will leave Boston and her marriage in 1883, taking three-year-old Angelina, *Nana*, with her, for the Midwest and work as theosophist and transcendentalist.

Archie will pay support, long for Sarah's return, rail (exposing his patriarchal contradictions) against Mrs. Stuart, Boston mental curist who, to Archie, was cause of Sarah's heart frailty: "to be called an oppressor when I had not scrupled to do all the housework … doing without a murmur everything which women ordinarily were accustomed to do—& all to save my wife—yes sir to be called an oppressor & the author of my wife's diseases—seemed more than I could or ought to bear." *May 1883*

"It is certainly a self-evident proposition that actions can have *moral* quality only on a supposition of freedom," wrote Sarah Stanley, transcendentalist, in *Personified Unthinkables* (1884), a book penned in Detroit where Stanley lived after leaving her marriage,

Single mothers had it hard then as now. As Nana grew, it seems her mother overhears remarks about the colour of her daughter's skin. She did not want Nana to suffer racism. But was sending Nana back to her father best for her daughter, or for her as white mother? For her mother's health (weak heart), or for her transcendentalist career?

Sarah will write Archie, 25 April 1887: "she needs that love and sympathy of one of her own race" and "just now I am not fit to have the care of her." Petitioning for divorce, she will wish only to be on friendly terms and keep in touch with her daughter. In May 1887, seven-year-old Nana will arrive in Boston by train, alone.

In letters, Sarah will urge Nana to "... improve in your writing as fast as you can, so as to write lessons and books when you get older, just as mama does. Then you can go to California, or Detroit, or anywhere in the world you wish." Sarah wrote on exotericism *learned from the decaying sacredotalisms of Egypt*, moving from Michigan to Kansas to San Francisco, LA, then Auckland, New Zealand in 1888 where she wrote as SE Stanley and from then on ~~left no record, no news.~~

Nana will keep her mother's 17 letters from 1887 all her life. "They repeatedly express the idea that separated loved ones fashion an enduring bond in the spiritual realm." (Maureen Honey, *Aphrodite's Daughters*)

Archie adores his daughter, will enrol her in elite schools with few Black students in Boston, in Washington, and will do his own work at a desk in the parlour, close to her, at home. The parlour!

Archie's anti-racist activism and work in New Negro diplomacy (after Abolition in 1865, the US appointed Black activists to diplomatic posts in colonies or Black-dominant countries, primarily Caribbean, to represent America, putting their activism at home on hiatus as diplomats must refrain from 'politics') will be key in Grimké's life and upbringing. Her father works from home, is present to Angelina as a mother, and only absent during his four years (1894–98) as American consul in the Dominican Republic, a time when Angelina will rebel against the uncle and aunt whose Washington home they shared, until her aunt begs she be sent away (sent she was, to board at Carleton Academy in Northfield, Minnesota ~~*where she fell in love with a girl*~~).

Her father's constant letters from the archipelagos led Grimké later to recall, "it was thought best not to take me down to [Santo Domingo] but so often and so vivid have I had the scene and life described that I seem to have been there too."

Grimké surely will know the freedom struggles waged in the Caribbean in the 17th through 19th centuries by slaves and masterless persons, mariners, free townfolk, breakaways, buccaneers, freebooters, maroons, scoundrels—folk Black and Brown and *polyglot*, unlike the enslaving whites. In microregional and cross-imperial incessant movements of commerce and dignity between shores south and north, they carried the call of revolutionary France through the archipelagos. In 1804, revolution in Haiti brought independence, ending chattel slavery there. In American slave states, northern free states, and on isles claimed by Euro-colonizers, news of revolution was frantically suppressed. To block reception of French ideals—*liberté, égalité, fraternité*—Black populations were disenfranchised of information by enslaving governments (including the new USA where speech will be free only for some). The archipelagos however teem with polylingual news, people moving, boats, harbours, flows, thinkings, and resolution. Later, in Grimke's time, the USA was in the Caribbean to exert influence to free up paths of commerce for American capital. (Archie deplored that his role meant defending planters and sugar barons ...)

Grimké's mother, Sarah Stanley Grimké, in her *First Lessons in Reality* (1886), was engaged in a more personal struggle, with congestive heart failure: "The appearance called Death is therefore only the last stage of the Lie of Physical Causation," she wrote. And: "... the visible effect of swallowing arsenic upon my body only expresses a more real effect, on the plane of finite mind, of the assassin Calumny upon my whole terrestrial usefulness and existence. However, when I grasp the meaning of the law of contradictories, and begin to know the esoteric life, I gradually come to know that the more powerless I am rendered on the lower plane, the more do I gain power on the true plane, if I but know how to use it."

Sarah returned ill from the Antipodes, it seems, to her parents' home in Michigan in 1897, then to San Diego where, without communicating with her daughter but including her in her last bequests, she died self-poisoned in 1898.

Angelina will then be 18. The news will reach her, and her small inheritance.

Surely Grimké, even out of curiosity, will have—at some point—read her mother's books ...

(Shhh, her father is home.)

Regard

Elisa Sampedrín

Where would I take decidability
if weary were a game I

could stop reviling?
Delirious in fields and

pondered by grasses, amid
timothy's green-grey feathers,

as if I were lying down every day
in my very creature

not abstract as endeavour but pure
homonym

or sexonym or synonym

For life?

Evanescence

Angelina Weld Grimké

You are like a pale purple flower
In the blue spring dusk
You are like a yellow star
Budding and blowing
In an apricot sky
You are like the beauty
Of a voice
Remembered after death
You are like thin, white petals
Falling
        And
                Floating
                        Down
Upon the white stilled hushing
        Of my soul.

It's 36°C in Montreal, a long head-swelling heatwave as I write. 44°C on the humidex. Watering plants at a neighbour's, I doggedly soak a fake orchid on a high shelf, thinking it real.

I seek out Grimké's poems silently, to hear her in anthologies: *Negro Poets and Their Poems* (ed. Robert T. Kerlin, 1923), *The New Negro* (ed. Alain Locke, 1925), *Caroling Dusk* (ed. Countee Cullen, 1927), and *Poetry of the Negro* (ed. Langston Hughes, 1949).

Kerlin says: "If hers should be called imagist poetry or not I cannot say, but I am certain that more vivid imaging of objects has not been done in verse by any contemporary. This, too, in stanzas that suggest in their perfection of form the work of the old lapidaries. Nor is there but a surface or formal beauty. There is passion, there is beauty of idea, the soul of lyric poetry is there as well as the form." He includes "Dawn," "A Winter Twlight," "The Puppet-Player," "The Want of You," "El Beso," "At the Spring Dawn," "To Keep the Memory of Charlotte Forten Grimké," and one stanza from "A June Song."

Dawn (2)

Grey trees, grey skies, and not a star;
Grey mist, grey hush;
And then, frail, exquisite, afar,
A hermit-thrush.

and from **El Beso**:

... Lure of you, eye and lip;
Yearning, yearning,
Languor, surrender;
Your mouth,
And madness, madness,
Tremulous, breathless, flaming,
The space of a sigh ...

37°C now, 45°C on the humidex today in Montreal.

4–13 July 1911 will also mark a record-breaking heatwave—in New England. Babies will not wake from naps, horses will collapse and die in the road, boats ooze liquid tar and sink in the harbour, boys fall under ice carts. People went insane, they will say.

5,000 will sleep outside in Boston Common to avoid suffocating inside human houses. Torpidity of limbs and thinking, the *no* of it.

Late on 10 July 1911, in this mind-fogging heat, Engineer Curtis in Philly or Washington will sign the register and board his engine to take the nine cars of the Federal Express, train 72, overnight sleeping car service (baggage cars, day coach, six Pullman sleepers) of the New York, New Haven and Hartford Railroad, to Boston.

It will not ar—

*Boston

~~*Charleston~~

*Washington

~~*Santo Domingo~~

That night, Angelina Weld Grimké, a Pullman passenger on train 72 from Washington, where she lives and teaches, will head to Boston, where she takes Harvard summer classes.

At 3:32 a.m. on 11 July 1911, Engineer Curtis, heat-doped, an hour late, loses 'situational awareness' or blanks on his order to slow to 15 mph and take the crossover from track 2 to 4 west of Bridgeport, CT to set off the US Fish Commission's baggage car of canned trout. Curtis hits the crossover at mainline speed, 60 mph, tumbling his train off the Fairfield viaduct in an agonizing roar of bending wood and metal.

The cars come to rest in a heap down an 18-foot embankment. Just two Pullman sleepers left on the track above.

Grimké may be in the forward one (the St. Louis Nationals baseball team are in the rear, and fine). Or in the sleeper just ahead, in the last car to leave the tracks and come to rest on top of the tumbled cars.

14 will die but she will not.

Her back ~~will be~~ is broken.

A baggage car of *canned trout*?

The delirium of heatwave.

In the 12 July 1911 *Philadelphia Inquirer*, the 42nd name on the list of injured passengers is *Miss Angelina Grimké.*

The photos in the paper—one day before the heatwave abated—are terrible. I look in dozens of images to see if I can find signs of Grimké but no … I learn later she is not able to rise alone and is in hospital with a broken back.

Today, track-embedded devices monitor speed and can stop a train via computer relay if the engineer fails to apply brakes on time. No such devices existed in 1911. Nor did any CTC manage signal lights remotely from a traffic control room. Engineers carried printed orders and, en route, read coloured signal tabs high on poles that had been set mechanically by station and yardmasters …

Yet electronic devices are no help if not activated. Railways have a long history of skimping on safety standards without breaking any laws. 'Loss of situational awareness' is a human failure. They just blame the engineers.

The heatwave is over.

Angelina Weld Grimké will write—share poetry, prose, drama, and publish often, before and during the Harlem Renaissance of the 1920s, will join Georgia Douglas Johnson's *S Street Salon* in Washington—yet her voice is not mechanically recorded; it is found in no sound archive though she lived until 1958.

Her 173 poems are more like Bishop's opus than like Rukeyser's. 31 poems were published, in 1902 or thereabouts and then in 1922 and 1927. Unlike Rukeyser, Grimké will not give out. Or give it in, inward, like Bishop.

Is it that she will give up? *Or give forward*, pointing to a future to which Archive is perhaps always blind and merely a force of power, *pointing to a future in a way my words and position as white lesbian inhibit me from seeing* ...

"Action, in so far as it engages in founding and preserving political bodies, creates the condition for remembrance, that is, for history," writes Hannah Arendt in "Vita activa...," Chapter 1 in *The Human Condition*, a touchstone of Western (white) thinking. Yes, it's anachronous to quote Arendt (Grimké died the year *THC* was first published in NYC), but the grip of racism *is* anachronous. The present tense *is* anachronous and therein lies pain for many of those who can only live the present. For Black and Brown bodies, time is out of joint.

The history we learn in schools is out of joint (thinking Ukraine as I write these words 2022.03.03 but also the archipelagos, and how in a history centred there the Americas read differently)

A sorrow and a silence will burn in Grimké's poetry, as well as kisses, light, longing. Addressing the conditions of reception as Rukeyser and Bishop never did, for she had no choice, her work is full of images of stark, leafless trees, pointing, scratching.

Emotion refracts through image; the image in Grimké is not a material fact observed (as in Bishop) but hovers on the page; its materiality turns the poem away from the material. Her aim will be to reflect 'moods,' the 'spiritual atmosphere.'

her mother

The Black Finger (first published in *Opportunity,* 1923)
Angelina Weld Grimké

I have just seen a beautiful thing
Slim and still,
Against a gold, gold sky,
A straight cypress,
Sensitive
Exquisite,

A black finger
Pointing upwards.
Why, beautiful still finger, are you black?
And why are you pointing upwards?

the future

Conditions of reception meant Grimké will not be able to speak in poetry to 'give back out,' not be able to readily address an American socius as an American (à la Rukeyser). Or turn poetry inward into the mysteries of the unexpected for an educated literary elite (Bishop). She will command neither the social nor the personal.

Because she necessarily speaks as Black *and* as a woman, the rostrum will be closed off to her, at least in part.

Closed like the *parloir* or speaking space in the set of *Rachel.*

Though closed off and airless, the parlour is safer than the street. Both more and less can be said on this. It's like a closet, but involuted: it makes speaking possible but the speaking is impossible for others to hear.

The Grimké family (for their own dignity) will perpetrate the idea that Angelina's mother had *abandoned* the family, was mentally ill, even 'incarcerated.' You can still read this here and there. Sarah in fact travelled freely, wrote, published, collaborated (at times with men who later erased her authorly name). What if Grimké, Black and lesbian—her poems speak of her love of women, and her father was vehemently against her love relationships, female and male—will simply choose after her father's death to live away from public view, to live and love in peace?

To commune with her mother as spirit creature? With her father (motherly) as spirit creature?

Why are you pointing upwards? *Cypress as healing and as mourning ...*

Agency is difficult to see and hear when you are outside it....

Grimké's long-awaited *Selected Works* (Oxford, 1991) does not collect her poems in her desired order, and (maddeningly) does not date them. The typeset margins seem sized for a smaller book. The editors' introduction speaks of the work she was shaping, then veers to situate her as historical, eliding her poetics and person.

Of the poems themselves, the editors note holographic variations but do not remark (for example) on her excision of a key line from the final version of "Evanescence." This information lies outside the book, in her archive or at https://washingtonart.com/beltway/grimke.html:

> "In her manuscripts, she makes various edits to colors and descriptions but the only substantive edit occurs after the line 'In an apricot sky' when she deleted 'Beyond the reach of black, black hands' which speaks directly to the intensity of her feelings of frustration." *Rebecca Villarreal*

"Caprichosa" and "El Beso" (1923) further estrange her desire for women by using *títulos en castellano*. Lesbian desire is so foreign to America, it can barely appear in English. It was seen as but a girlish intimacy that imitates/ precedes the 'propriety' of heterosexual union.

Will some future bring Grimké into the archive of a Poetry Room, she and other women of the Harlem Renaissance, into the publicly available 'Poetry' 'Room' 'Archive'? What even *are* these words? Will we hear their voices? They are already always there. *Will the archive itself shift and break so they are audible?*

Angelina Weld Grimké in this book appears inevitably in the pattern of my voice, which is no voice. A white voice. I have no other.

In an apricot sky
~~Beyond the reach of black, black hands~~
You are like the beauty
Of a voice
Remembered....

The *fenda* is a real place and it is *so f*king gay*. ES
(poetry grow/s here)
Which 'we' am I a part of? "To what do I belong in this present?"

Grimké will have spent the remaining painful months of 1911 at home in a body cast to heal her back, her father nursing her. *Pain felt by the body is thus a task for history.** A gym teacher, she is strong—a resistance perhaps to her mother's uncoupling of physical from spiritual health. I wonder if it weren't one way for a lesbian to teach in the company of women, for sports were segregated by gender. After growing up in mixed but mostly white society, Grimké will teach at Black schools in Washington's segregated system. She will leave a school where she is at odds with the Principal who accuses her, a Phys Ed teacher, of trying to *insinuate herself* into a job teaching English. Literature and writing she loves. She will defy administrators when she needs to.

In 1926, at 46, Angelina Weld Grimké will stop teaching due to 'ill health.' Freed from classrooms and unsupportive administrations, she will publish frequently over the next year.

Two scant years later, she will nurse her father through his final illness. The presence in the Washington Grimké house of the rules-driven Francis James Grimké, her father's brother, Christian minister (and master tea brewer), whose Calvinist rigidity Nana fled as a teen (Minnesota), will not deter her. Her father she adores.

One month after Archibald Grimké dies in Washington in February 1930, his daughter will be gone. The family home means no more to her. She belongs to poetry. With her inheritance, she will move to New York City. To write.

to redefine her migration not as a 'giving up,' and her

silence as

archipelago:

a future she will grant to others to fulfill

, a world tree

, healing tree
willow, cherry, oak, birch
human nervature
tree of light

(arduous)
(ardorous)

pointing upwards

My own mother on wanting no tomb: If you want me you can find me in the trees.

Newly arrived in New York in spring 1930, Roaring Twenties over and Great Depression in course, Nana, Angelina, will be 50. Even today a woman of 50 is unwelcome as job applicant, too old to be 'the new,' and AWG will still have pain from the train wreck in 1911. It's hard when in pain to present yourself as young. Back pain is worse when you sit at a desk; it radiates through the organs.

Angelina will live 28 more years and never publish again.

The heatwave?

What heatwave.
That grating tearing sound of metal? The burnt smell of twisted wood?

We don't remember.

It's over.

shoe

Will Grimké *love* in New York? Or *fall in love*? She is as used to *unrequited love* as Elizabeth Bishop was to the requited, I will wager. By the mid 1930s, friends will still try to convince her to marry (a man) to avoid loneliness. In the early 1900s, she'd considered it; her diaries comment then on a few men, although with ambivalence.

Letters to her in the 1930s will indicate a suspicious woman who does not easily retain friends, drives people away. She will travel nearby on vacation but mostly will keep to her New York apartment. A letter to a friend in 1936 finds her at the Massachusetts seaside, fearing a return to the "loneliness and uselessness" of New York.

Angelina. You are of the future but cannot reach it. Chaos-monde.

In the 1950s, she will at times be seen—elderly, in her 70s—buying groceries. Her obituary will appear in the *New York Times* on 11 June 1958, headlined: "Poet, Ex Teacher, 78."

It will be said somewhere that many of her belongings were put out on the street. On the curb, amid the piles or boxes, were there her mother's books?

> *Personified Unthinkables* (Detroit, 1884)
> *First Lessons in Reality* (LA, 1886)
> *The Light of Egypt, or the Science of the Soul and the Stars Vol. 1* with Thomas H. Burgoyne, published in 1889 as authored by 'Zanoni' (reprinted with additions in 1901 after SSG's death, it will be attributed solely to Burgoyne)
> *A Tour Through the Zodiac* (1900)

What is difficult, the difficult thing, would be to understand that what is proper to us, what is natural for us, is the impropriety that a person is, our being *alien*, our being other, our irremediable freedom. And live the consequences of that difficulty.

Chus Pato

from O natal para o poema, *September 2019, tr. EM*

O difícil, o difícil sería comprender que o propio, o natural para nós, é a impropiedade do que unha é, o seu ser alleo, o seu ser outro, a súa liberdade sen remedio. E vivir as consecuencias desa dificultade.

Y vivir las consecuencias de esa dificultad. It could be that Angelina speaks to her mother. She will keep her letters. For both of them in their different ways, the physical points to the spiritual.

How can you forget a mother with whom you lived and who cherished you until you were seven? (Bishop's mother too left the house when B. was seven and B. never forgot.)

Grimké's mother disbelieved in the physical realm yet let race and racism, a plague of the physical realm, divide her from her daughter. Esotericists like Sarah would laud an all-inclusive 'human race,' yet in their works and acts this humanity would become whiter and whiter. Sarah Stanley Grimké acquiesced to this.

Think about psyche silence natality materiality the sitting room the crashed train the fall down the embankment

the torsioned back
the cure the mental cure

House me and waken me

darling shoe

[my mother, white settler immigrant from an earlier space/time and from the old religion, walks in the woods of this book and no stick cracks underfoot. The leaves listen to her for she is these leaves. She has an absolute physicality that recognizes the parity of all things: *the grass is writing too, you know*, she says to me, her voice defiant—poetry? what good is a poetry that relies on human exceptionalism … she's right … AWG too knew this, all her trees, her dark trees …]

In commentary on her poems, Grimké is seen not as *important*, but *historical.* Interesting for her historical presence but not for what she will bring to poetry itself.

To look at *why* she will not produce 'important poems': hers is a voice curtailed. A Black and lesbian voice marked by strictures against loving women. Hard enough for a woman, harder for a lesbian, even harder for a Black woman. Nigh on impossible for a Black lesbian, even of a certain education and class. Only later will (white?) critics include her as "poet of Sapphic modernism" alongside Amy Lowell, Gertrude Stein, HD, *integrating her 'into' a field in which her difference still vanishes.*

It is in Washington in 1902–1910, teaching gym and English, summering in Boston and learning at Harvard, where she will write her best work, ardent, linking Nature to Black desire, to secret kisses. Her earlier poetry will convey emotional force in a multitude of ways, innocent, not worn down in affective power.

It's rhyme that is emotional (just as for EB rhyme is "mystical"). Is rhyme a way to say everything she will not say directly? As sound pattern?

Rhyme beckons her reader through, in a caress of similarity, of words touching other words. Sound is in the chests: heart sound.

Is rhyme an embrace?

In the time of Covid, I think we can understand rhyme as suture between reflected physical body and celestial form

Her work could enter the socius here, *my socius*: breathing.

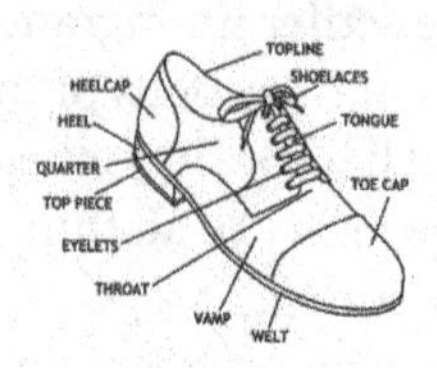

The year Grimké dies in New York, Hannah Arendt will publish *The Human Condition* in that same city. The book posits a human exceptionalism arising from natality viewed as fount of possibility and choice and individuation, and lauds the "fact of being born" that Angelina Grimkë will involute in her life and work because the racial violence that founds the American socius forbids this choice arising to racialized persons and thus makes it unfree.

In fact, natality will *not* produce its freeing effects for every human. The linking of natality to freedom hides the perilous condition in which natality obliges so many to begin and live.

In the silence of the archive:
(there is a glaring flaw in Arendt, I see this even as I read her,
our *impropriety* its fissure)
(a howling wind

Homi Bhabha *The Location of Culture:*

"It is that Third Space, though unrepresentable
in itself, which constitutes the diSCUrSIVe condiOons of enuncl-atici

ii !J ensure-ffial' ffie MmeanJilg'"and w;ymbOIS of cul , ; ;,(,

P fli.ii tY; I!i T Y iDli!!@i ,$\ ap. r9Rria g,

tr I Je..Q, 1"!'!}\is ori ed C\J:ld. t:e!:l.d ..an e|w..,"

Deuteronomy into Colonization

Elisa Sampedrín

I gave up singing the alphabet
Accents released me
from the start of memory's wound

to its apex
Oh fearful symmetry!

I went over to the bark of trees
The places where insects
full of lust were chiding
the lords of Deuteronomy

The final syllable
and as I put the accent

on that syllable
quiet as the birds are quiet
ardent as an insect is

electricity in the wires above us
electricity in the ~~R~~
                                        shore

("It is that Third Space, though unrepresentable in itself, which constitutes the discursive conditions of enunciation that ensure that the meaning and symbols of culture have no primordial unity or fixity; that even the same signs can be appropriated, translated, rehistoricized, and read anew." HB, *LoC*, copy-pasted from a scan)

Futilité (2) p. 107

Angelina Weld Grimké, tr. EM

Quand j'étais jeune et innocente,
        Je filais souvent en douce
Dans la nuit silencieuse
        En cherchant de ressentir.

Maintenant dans ma vieillesse si sage
        Parmi les ombres croissantes,
Ô ! Comment elle me manque, la fille
        Qui cherchait il y a si longtemps.

~~Holographic variations: I used to slip into},~~
~~{When I was young and innocent/ I used to rise an … [illegible]~~
~~/ Into the night quiet}, {~~
~~To suffer love},~~ {To suffer love}.

winter came, delight!)

(but covid sroard)

(I never threw away my mother's shoes)

ES

Betanzos, 1955–Montreal 20_

from “Grail,” for *Norma Cole*

For what are we but
“not innocent”
In-innocent and
not bystanders

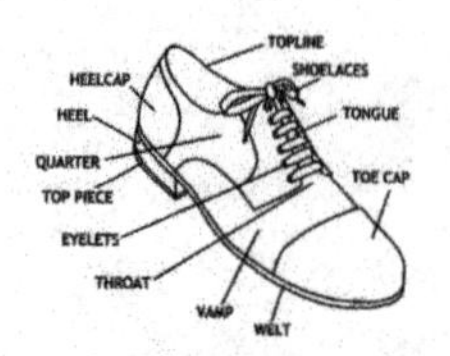
TOPLINE
HEELCAP
SHOELACES
HEEL
TONGUE
QUARTER
TOP PIECE
TOE CAP
EYELETS
THROAT
VAMP
WELT

Exhale / Énonce
(emit's breathhold)

How to write poetry

There was nothing different
or it was the same

I had grief at a window
meaning
we had grief, there was no window

Grief was something we "had"?
We ached the long way round
Little fists of bright leaves emerged
                    up and down the straights
                    of branches

It was spring, an infection
ran amok in persons known
not known

Persons on the street vanished
and returned
between equinox and solstice
Droves like us, we said
Droves like us

and a woman on a third-floor balcony in the wind,
holding up a blue & yellow watering can.

Spring Hay + Watch

1

I dreamed of peeing and woke up dry
Words of geese replaced geese in the air too
Their chests of perfect grey down
in the air
point where geese point, honking as they fly
one wing toward each ocean

In my mind waking up
Words of geese
flying ↖↘ air

Something about geese and air
When I move in air I displace air
Corporeally
Yes really
When geese move in air
air condenses inside their chests

That's why they fly
That's why I'm grounded

Odd patter of morning in my mind waking up
Old hay uncut by the fence posts
appears from snow later as bent blades
yellow
in spring

(the design of the room)
(the exile of populations following on war)
(cuneiform record in old Sumerian)
(arroy)

2

Beauty = Kant

Sublime = Longinus

Voice, timbre = space, light

The radicality of forms in forms, forms through forms, the radicality of just
using a form

"Lost her mother's watch"

Spivak: "it is the failure of the Kantian sublime"

So I looked for women (Rukeyser, Bishop, Grimké) who had made and were formed by migrations, and who were in some way marked 'questionably' by the socius, and I examined what I could of the forms and shapes of their migrations-

-having just translated Rosalía de Castro, modernist before modernism

Catalogue

I end up not sure,
or aching.
Bees bees and bees!

The goodbye was certain,
glad (for each other),
not tremulous.

The curtain not shut,
did not descend
on any stage.

In the dark we could still see
the sets, rolled
offstage in *panneaux*

and lined up in the wings
post-applause
like giant books in a library.

None of them in circulation.
None even in storage.
Catalogued, of course.

For posterity? Oh
no.
For the present (tense).

So many notes, set
down in crimped rows to be
legible to a future

are never again read.
Ardent was our sowing!
Bees bees and bees!

Alborada*

Rosalía de Castro, 1863

I.

Go now dark-
ness—Go get go-
ing—Come on sun-
rise—Keep on open-
ing—Your face whose sm-
ile—Scares off shadows!!!

Sing!…
Songbird sing-
ing—From branch to branch-
ing—So that sun may be ris-
ing—Over verdant moun-
tains—Over peaks so ver-
dant—Delighting grass-
blades—Delighting spring-
waters!…

Sing, delightful songbird,
Sing!
Sing so corn will grow.
Sing!
Sing so light will listen to you.
Sing!
Sing that night has fled.

Dark night
Comes then,
And lingers long
With its mantle
Of sadness,

* Rosalía: *What I found hardest in writing this alborada was my wish that it emerge with a musical flow. I managed this, but at the cost of poetry. It could not have been done in any other way; the music moves with such a strange air it is hard to put any words to it at all.*

With spells
And frights,
Prophet
Of sorrows,
Sanctuary
Of mourning,
Shelter
Of regrets,
Protector
Of all misfortune,
Leave!...

So that sweet sunrise
May colour the sky
And the trees
It swoons to love,
With a semblance
Of gold and silver
Dipped softly
In scarlet.
With robes
Of diamond
It embroiders
The loving sun
Between waves
Of crystal.

Leave!...
Mistress of all misfortune,
For the sun
Shines already
On the beach shells,
For the light
Of day
Dresses the earth in delight,
For the sun
Melts cold frost with love.

II.

Pale sun-
rise—Now arriv-
ing—And in door-
ways—Enters call-
ing—The yet-sleep-
ing—Now await-
ing—Your splendour!...

Tint ...
Of gorgeous dawn
Extends
Caressing
Into windows,
Where the sun
Hovers also,
While far out
At sea it stretches
And flares up in
Living fire,
Then rises,
Fugitive,
Sad wandering
Splendour.

Cantor
Of breezes,
Delightful songbird,
Sing,
Sing so corn will grow.
Cantor
Of sunrise,
Delightful lover,
To the young girls it says
The golden sun is out.

For the piper,
Washed freshly,
Well dressed,

Combed neatly,
Along with
His bagpipe
Is at the door!...
Wow!...

If in saying
What it says to you,
It resounds,
It resounds
In a sunrise
So beloved
By young girls
Wild for singing,
Wild for dancing,
So lively they are;
And by old crones
So delighted,
Who make
Merriment reign.

Up up!
All you girls in the village!
For the sun
And sunrise are here to wake you:
Up up!
Get up, you crazy youngsters!
Let's whoop-it-
Up—And yodel *oh! la! la!!!...*

from *Galician Songs (1863)*
tr. Erín Moure (2016)

Grail

for Norma Cole

There is no grail
But poetry makes
of us a grail every
moment

Et ceci, dans
plusieurs langues

For what are we but
"not innocent"
In-innocent and
not bystanders

Our trials are yet
unexpunged from history
Racism and misogyny
still haunt us

She Norma Cole showed me
desire's map is possible
and must
include   Tap Tap
birds

If there were
a poem of courage
Poem making thick of courage
its own ways
To weight courage
in a generation

An expertise of questions
and syllables
fondly
The way music is flattered
to be known as music

2

Intent I was on learning
"something"
Norma helped me
with her way of
listening always
at the end of questions
(not answering
but letting my mouth form
syllables

slowly)—a sensation
not unpleasant
"Not to be interrupted"
is so rare

Her smile as I am doing so
Or for any other
who may be reaching

for I am but an equal
voicing
in-inocente de calquera
pensamento
se non é: *acoller*

not wanting but
Tap Tap
Listen

abeirada
within this a-
grail

8 August 1980, 2:40 a.m. PDT. 16 cars of VIA transcontinental train #4 derailed at Thunder River, BC. *Awoke from sleep knowing the car was in the air, its metal screaming as the frame was bending, rivets popping through the paint, and a terrifying noise below of wooden ties gratering and splintering to slow us to a stop. No one died. Yet the noise alters the cells. One never forgets.*

The sleeping car that hangs off the end of the cliff is called, curiously, *Endcliffe*. An E-type sleeper, never returned to service. The car frame bent and roomette door stuck; in trapped panic I manage to tug it ajar and take a sledgehammer from a hand outside in a corridor full of smoke and grit. With it, I break the window. After pushing blankets out over jagged glass and tying bedsheet to a handrail, I shift backwards out into the darkness of the steep riverbank and slide down the sheet (hand blisters). The wood in the foreground is ties. I'm in jeans (my PSA uniform skirt didn't make sense climbing out a window) and the top half of my uniform. To get to the rear of the train and the passengers in those cars until the rescue train came to get us (impossible to get us all up the wet bank to the buses they first sent), I crawl on my stomach under this car. All day long, back and forth, between two worlds, one shattered with passengers wandering draped in blankets, one simply in hiatus, its persons drinking in the tail-end lounge car.

Loam

An animal crept up my chest at noon
and I forbade it

Watched it animal-sit and wait
for me to give in

to distraction or abeyance
far over the ditches

where light is
light came shining

leaves shone at their frittered edges
light + leaves

what is the relation

how does light travel
and leaves
and the animal
leaving

and the loam
—now that it's needed—
it's dark here

where is the loam

Manners

purity
not maybe

sordid manners
in hotels

my armature
incantatory

just
mark
time

2

thick-neck
herefords

bees quizzing
flowers

yellow spikes
green door

earth's a
good planet

to say goodbye to
or just goodbye

Iteration

I gave up my breath
for an iteration

My "I" for a
wound

My face for a consensual
fabric

Tuesday, Wednesday
Friday

Fake hedonists with
bucolic daydreams

"I" am not "you"

I still have names
for disabeyance

watching
fireworks light up the sky

in closets

where no one
is mean

Masked Up

If this
is to stop that

from ferrying through
a population

The impregnanc/e
of hurt

The boundary
not marked by twine

Twice-fed
burped   lazy

Rosacea on a cheek-
bone

jutted
under wayworn eyes

To ensure
no one is infected

or because of me
might hurt or die

Rotters
Synaesthesia

will not save or
forgive you

Artful I sing in
singing's absence

Pass that mask to me yes
I'll put it on

Con<u>tra</u>vention
for Fred Wah

All that jazz
'd up
contravention

Practising here again
Alone-itude
in an apartment

Even in that word
art lies
its immediate aporia

upholding

spent factions
deer or does
or any other passage

rosehips at sunset
not quite ripe yet
for bears

whose doings
echo sunset

he**art**en me
still

Glebe

this is the final greeting, which we bring every day

On the pavement
a little bird
who did not make it

Stripped raw, as if for
swimming

Throat open, as if for
food
beak-lipped yellow

not quotidian
ever
tiny gorgeous
hatchling

Fallen as if for
always

fallen
backward
Featherless wing bones
sidelong

A skin spendthrift
once-bird
once-garden

absent from
humidity's plenitude

not reticent
in any manner

Insects chiming
over its
soft sigh

Conundrum

1

To be and my aversions
medicated

Sorry some days I am here
but banking

(as in flight)

on tomorrow's

utterances, oh my
friends

scrappy
really scrappy

2

What if there were juice or jam
I lean in, hopeful

Did you hear
my
subjunctive?

3

Either way
my conundrum

still silence

I don't know why
poetry

made me like this

4

writing down

crayon/papier
pencil/paper
lapis/papel

moving stairs

between floors

in a library

Synonym

My language is older
than the language
spoken in your language

in your language
some words do not exist
that in my language
still persist

the urge to write at my ripe age
depends on them

your language is full of
clauses placed so that
they alter time

an arm belongs instead
to a flower
leaving a person wounded

I am hearing a train go by
metal wheels on metal rails

I first wrote "metal word"
and yet lucidity, as in the phrase
"I'll knock your lights out"
where lights
mean thinking, mean
the brain

speaking as it is spoken
here
older than any language

leaving a person wounded
leaving a flower

Dust

Walking this road, one day
I'll be dust in it too, I
don't mind

Dust in the road
same trees over it

Winter snow or hot sun
View or no view, I
don't mind

In trunks high above
perch *picapaus*

lifting their feathered
heads sideways, all
messed up on top

then back to the tree
to get on with a day's work

cracking open insects

bark busting

hamm*ering* away

Eau Claire

after seeing The Demonstration *by Coco Guzmán*

It will be the end of
living memory.
My mother whom I hear in me
as ancient person will disappear from
the earth
and its beings and its
lights.

Grass, hair, bones.
A cricket singing on a lawn in
evening, five p.m.

2

Wind, branch, the insect's DNA in the light.
Flatness of the lawn.

3

In the dream, my body watched my body
entering the flames.
Behind it the buildings seem uninhabited.
Language is a prosthesis:
my tongue and mouth Galician.

Perhaps afterward I will enter
the body of another as ancient person.
Teeth, fluid, bone.

4

The clay fish teeming, by *Coco Guzmán*.
Their Greek frieze.
Bodies composed perfectly,

sexed and intersexed.
The vagina of the powerful man
The breasts of the minister.
The tissue of the lungs.

5

The fish too are naked of sexes,
are sardinhas, sardiñas.
Their shadows on the floor are
scraps of light, blurred.

The gallery is full and
empty and
I am long   gone.

The waters flow   clear
and   soundless

past   *Eau claire* where

by the Elbow current

in a minute I'll be here

arrived in the old hospital

out of my mother's blood

to be given

a name

Spindle

I wake up today and it's November.
The month of my mother.
I carry some of her cancer on my arms
to help her.
She says this is unnecessary.
She is drawing jets in a notebook
with a pencil, concentrating on
the exact shadow

down one side of a fuselage.

As if she were her own sons as children,
in a love of modernity's machines.
And I her daughter, her one daughter
lifting water
in a drawn vessel
carrying her cancer on my own arms

which she says (looking up, then down
to the tip of the pen again)

is unnecessary.

~~Soon, all of us will get onto her aeroplane~~
~~without suitcases or maps~~
~~and fly away.~~

Eight Tests for Breathing

Erin Mouré

from Domestic Fuel, *1985*

1

Stoop of the bronchial body
in the red brick building
Philosophy
To use well what is
if it is little

Say only meaning & go on
The heart can't read possibility
sick & tired
hurts me

2

Shut up if I do skip words
I can't breath_*
I can't stop
breathing

3

Little & sick again
a dressing gown with red cats
Billy & Kenny
my brothers
their voices at distances, high giggles
I hang on to them, home from school, unseen
Another day past
I want them to argue
so I'll hear them longer
before they're gone
screen door slammed again

4

Bricks the building block of language
Grew up learning it
My mother gave me words
from the torn linoleum where she stood
before the sink
Later she worked outside
against my father's wishes
She bought linoleum & a new sink
I don't recognize
I can't believe I learned to read
there

5

Short lines
mince words
Struggle to get up & pee again
hot body waiting to catch breath
in the greying hall

6 *End The Arms Race Day, 24 April 1982*

In the North where I am my life
solves with little pain
I think careful in my airless brain
communicate, try
Bloody Americas
who kill the witnesses, the mouths blown up
I can't breathe enough
to speak against human enemies
The armaments
If I'm sick
& don't say
Absolve me

7

In a far-off room
my family, eating dinner
The sound of their plates, mouths, evening
converse

My place empty

The windows of my bed
too high
The bricks darkening
Cool air outside, & family, & me
craving speech like all others

I want to grow up now
& breathe easy

Say it's worth it, kiddo

8

There is measure
the throat takes
& knows not
A measure like a step back
on a scaffold

These nights I risk to breathe
I dream
the workmen take down the scaffolding
around my building
red brick
Turning the braces, opening vise
upon vise
carefully wrenching the rods apart,
the boards that held them
stacked dirty
So few words
Little breath

The same old lungs' hurt & damage
& can't be cured
The breath there is
as the hands flutter
is poetry

Outside the poem, the scaffolds down at last
The building stands cleanly

View Court Housing Co-op, Vancouver, 1982

XXXII

César Vallejo

999 calorías.
Rumbbb … Trrrapprrr rrach … chaz
Serpentínica *u* del bizcochero
engirafada al tímpano.

Quién como los hielos. Pero no.
Quién como lo que va ni más ni menos.
Quién como el justo medio.

1,000 calorías.
Azulea y ríe su gran cachaza
el firmamento gringo. Baja
el sol empavado y le alborota los cascos
al más frío.

Remeda al cuco: Roooooooeeeis …
tierno autocarril, móvil de sed,
que corre hasta la playa.

Aire, aire! Hielo!
Si al menos el calor (__________ Mejor
no digo nada.

Y hasta la misma pluma
con que escribo por último se troncha.

Treinta y tres trillones trescientos treinta
y tres calorías.

de *Trilce* (1922)

XXXII On Heat

tr. ES (in June)

999 calories.*
Rhummmbl … Trapperrr ach … chazz
Meandering **u** of the brio*uuu*che vendor
spinfaffling deep into the ear.

Here's to ice cubes! But no.
Here's to whoever budges the least.
Here's to the happy medium.

1,000 calories.
The gringo firmament goes blue and laughs up
its massive languor. Down
goes the duped sun and jaggles those noggins
most chill.

Go cuckoo: Rooooooo iiiis …
soft roadway, thirst-rippled,
heads all the way to the beach.

Air, air! Ice!
If only the heat (_________ Best
that I shut up.

Even the pen-tip
I'm writing with finally goes bust.

Thirty-three trillion three-hundred thirty
and three calories.**

* 999. *Measure of heat needed to raise temperature of 1g water by 1°C.*
** 33,000,000,000,000,333. *Too bloody hot on this planet & just June 23.*
I'm out of here.

Churl

I went through the jungles
Earls ate my hair
ate my hands

Sparrows saved me
Only the sparrows came clean

There were sediments not sentiments
I was handless
and hairless

a grub or hatchling
(stubborn and puckish)

Under the conditions
which were their conditions
which were Earl conditions

could I grow arms?
could I grow tresses?

or could I (dream on)
under my sparrow conditions
grow feathers?
grow wings?

Upon hearing of the letter "Justice and Open Debate" in Harper's Magazine, *7 July 2020, signed by 148 luminaries, who while saying good things don't acknowledge people and groups who have always been silenced/rebuffed by the system of 'open debate,' always been taken less seriously. As if Earls, a low rung of nobility, argue to maintain their privileges of breath in the face of the rest of human being, whom they produce—nameless—as Churls.*

Stor- of the shrou-

A book so new
that when opened for the first time
it smells like bandages.

A book that
when opened
smells like bandages.

The adoration of one king, another king, a queen throwing up
beside the bed,

her children crying beneath a painting
hungry

Alone in the house all afternoon
ceiling fan quietly turning
Sinking my nose in a book still new

Whose pages   opened outward

Smell just like

leaving the hospital after the

acci/dent

(don't worry, nothing "else" matters
I'm here with her waiting
I think we're okay)

Yield

The forks the sea has
tarnished are silver, not tin
We let ourselves outside,
it rains, we go in

In partial abeyance
a jukebox gone still
I'm off *passeando*
for words where words will

Mastery in poems was
maestria back when
A cut in a finger
lean wolf in a den

Poe, boy in a sandwich
cow lost in the field
If I can wake better
words might to me

yield

a fetter a tatter
a trail a torr-ent
of water down hillside
to where it would went

sing to me *Матусю*
sing me of Ukraine
sing me in your darkness
sing sing it's no game—

for every body

Her Pharmacopœia

BREATH can be archived, but not non-breath.
Can listening be archived? It is what answers breath. Non-breath is where life is, yes, impossible, but there is too a non-breath in which— we listen— for the breath— we barely— can but— ho— pe to hear.

from a notebook
(whose? EM's? ES's?)

How to 'un-realize' the poem?

Hither lies time's threshold (ici se trouve le seuil du temps) and we see it shift our step and breath, not in writing but *in reading*. Reading is the interface that both stops and starts time. Reading answers breath. Reading is a kind of act prior to writing for it urges writing to come to be, *so that we can read it.* Reading goes beyond the book.

The body is its archive.

or it has no archive
or: its reason is not archive

ES or *EM*

J'ai tenté de fournir une forme à une écriture de la différence culturelle au sein de la modernité qui soit inamicale aux frontières binaires : qu'elles soient entre passé et présent, dedans et dehors, sujet et objet, signifiant et signifié.

Homi Bhabha, *Les lieux de la culture*
(a cultural lag brings this book into the present in French only decades later)

My body: my archive.

ENDNOTES TO THE TEXTS AND POEMS

v

Didi-Huberman, Georges. *Gestes d'air et de pierre*. Paris: Éditions de Minuit, 2016, 14.

vii

Harris, Claire. From "Of Survival" in *The Conception of Winter*. Toronto: Williams-Wallace, 1989, 48.

xii

Poem by EM, from stone 'rest stop' in Cimetière Notre Dame des Neiges, Montréal. Approximate location 45°29'54.6"N 73°36'37.0"W. *Cemetery does not take care of them as of 2022, so these poem rest stops may vanish one day.*

2

Bhabha, Homi. *The Location of Culture*. NYC: Routledge, 1994, 351.

11

Chi Ha, Kim. "Rice is heaven"; 밥이 하늘입니다. Tr. Rev. Dr. Hyuk Cho, United Church of Canada, 2005. https://united-church.ca/worship-special-days/asian-heritage-month-1. Accessed July 2022.

> Rice is heaven,
> Because heaven cannot be possessed by one
> Rice must be shared with each other.
> Rice is heaven.
> Just as together we view the stars in heaven,
> Rice must be shared by all.
> When rice is eaten
> Heaven enters the body.
> Rice is heaven.
> *Ah-ah!* Rice must be shared!

13

Jeffers, Robinson. "Shine, Perishing Republic" first read in 1971 in the Dent Canadian school anthology *Impact* (ed. William Eckersley, 1968) in the "Protest" section, just before Kenneth Patchen's "The Orange Bears."

15

Rukeyser, Muriel. Quote from a 1940 letter to Louis Untermeyer starting "I believe in poetry," from *Muriel Rukeyser and Documentary* by Catherine Gander. Edinburgh: U Press, 2013, 131.

16

Moure, Erín. "I Learned Something About Writing from You in the Sports Pages of the Montreal Gazette: A Conversation with Joshua Lovelace, September 28, 1994" in *My Beloved Wager*. Edmonton: NeWest Press, 2009, 79–86.

17

Moure, Erín. "Seebe," *WSW*. Montreal: Véhicule Press, 1989, 81–84.

20

Camera Three, CBS, 1 August 1965, w. poets James Dickey, Peter Viereck, host James MacAndrew. "Travelling Poets" episode. Available online.

21

Rukeyser, Muriel. "Flying to Hanoi," *Collected Poems of Muriel Rukeyser*. Pittsburgh: U Pittsburgh Press, 2006, 508. The visual treatment of the poem is not part of the original.

Rilke, Rainer María. "Archaïscher Torso Apollos," usually translated as "Archaic Torso of Apollo," regardless of translator. Available online.

Martin Heidegger talked about Van Gogh's shoes (the ones he painted, and perhaps wore) in his essay "The Origin of the Work of Art." Heidegger's description of the shoes as women's shoes (they are peasant boots and not gendered really) is the subject of much contention among critics. The essay was first published in German in 1950 and is in *Martin Heidegger: The Basic Writings*. New York: HarperCollins, 2008, 143–212, tr. David Farrell Krell. A sentence from the Heidegger essay prompted the drawing of a shoe in *The Elements*, a drawing that has infiltrated this book too.

22

Rukeyser, Muriel. *The Life of Poetry*. 1949, reissued 1996 by Paris Press (now Wesleyan U Press). Reviewed 14 April 1997 by Eileen Myles in *The Nation*, "Fear of Poetry: Muriel Rukeyser, The Life of Poetry."

Rukeyser, Muriel. "Letter to the Front," *Collected Poems*, op. cit., 235.

23

Paz, Octavio. *Early Poems 1935–1955*, tr. Rukeyser et al., Indiana U Press, 1963; NYC: New Directions, 1973. In her 1963 foreword, MR speaks of meeting Paz and starting to translate him in 1944.

24

Paz, Octavio. "The Street," tr. Octavio Paz and Muriel Rukeyser, from R's *The Green Wave*, NYC: Doubleday, 1948, 53. (The version in *Early Poems* is revised.) "La Calle," by Octavio Paz, *Early Poems 1935–1955*, 70.

26

Paz, Octavio. "Poet's Epitaph," tr. Paz and Rukeyser, from R's *The Green Wave*, 50. "Epitafio para un poeta," by Octavio Paz, *Early Poems 1935–1955*, 14.

30

Yes, there is a reference to Canadian poet Fred Wah concealed here. Always!

31

Bishop, Elizabeth. epigraph from "Filling Station," *POEMS*. NYC: Farrar, Straus and Giroux, 2015, 125.

32

Bishop, Elizabeth. Letter to Frani Blough, 1 January 1935, *One Art: Letters*, ed. Robert Giroux. NYC: Farrar, Straus and Giroux, 1995, 29.

33

Tóibin, Colm. *On Elizabeth Bishop*. Princeton, NJ: Princeton U Press, 2015, 143.

Paz, Octavio. "Elizabeth Bishop, or the Power of Reticence," *Elizabeth Bishop and Her Art*, ed. L. Schwartz and S. P. Estess. Ann Arbor: U Michigan Press, 1983, 211.

*Moure, Erín. "Tr-lating Wilson Bueno," *The Elements*. Toronto: Anansi, 2019, 27.

34

Bishop, Elizabeth, on the glass eye is from "Writing Poetry Is an Unnatural Act," in *PROSE* by Elizabeth Bishop. NYC: Farrar Straus and Giroux, 2011, 331.

*Bishop's opening words at a reading at the Guggenheim Museum in NYC, after an introduction by Robert Lowell commending her "famous eye," May 1969. Online at https://magazine.nd.edu/stories/my-search-for-elizabeth-bishop/.

36

*It strikes me that 'wearing x out' today may mean 'going outside in x,' not 'using x until its fabric frays beyond use.' *I think now of Van Gogh's shoes, and Heidegger.*

Bishop, Elizabeth. "… wheezing and reading …" from letter to Anne Stevenson, 6 March 1964. In *PROSE* by Elizabeth Bishop, op.cit., 428–29.

39

Winslow, Anne, ed. *Trial Balances: An Anthology of New Poetry*. Intro by Marianne Moore. NYC: Macmillan, 1935.

40

Paz, Octavio. "Elizabeth Bishop, or the Power of Reticence," op. cit.

41

The Bishop line is from "The Moose," *POEMS*, op. cit., 189. The highway from Great Village to Boston in her day went along the Fundy Shore, then north into the woods from Parrsboro and on into New Brunswick (the Trans-Canada Highway was built later). As for smell: we need breath to smell anything, so breath is present in this line.

42

Bishop, Elizabeth. "To the Admirable Miss Moore," *Edgar Allen Poe & The Jukebox: Uncollected Poems, Drafts and Fragments*, ed. Alice Quinn. NYC: Farrar, Straus and Giroux, 2006, 84.

Bishop, Elizabeth. "Visits to St. Elizabeths," *POEMS*, op. cit., 131.

43

Porter, Eleanor H. *Pollyanna*. NYC: LC Page, 1913. Classic in Bishop's time, and mine.

44

Cole, Norma. *Where Shadows Will: Selected Poems 1988–2008*. SF: City Lights, 2009.

Cabrera, Lydia, and Édouard Glissant. *Trembling Thinking*. NYC: Americas Society, 2018.

Pato, Chus. Of the four books named, *Sonora* has not yet appeared in Galician. The other three are tr. by EM into English.

Césaire, Aimé. *Cahier d'un retour au pays*, 1939 (and Wesleyan U Press, 2013, a bilingual edition as *The Original Notebook of a Return to the Native Land*, tr. A. James Arnold).

45

Ajens, Andrés. "Short/Stor-," tr. EM, in Chain #10, 2003; *So-lair Storm* (to come).

48

Bishop, Elizabeth. "Under the Window, Ouro Prêto," *POEMS*, op.cit., 175.

49

Bishop, Elizabeth. "House Guest," *POEMS*, op. cit., 170.

White, Gillian. *Lyric Shame: The "Lyric" Subject of Contemporary American Poetry*. Cambridge, MA: Harvard U Press, 2014, 58.

50

Novoneyra. Uxío. Poem from *The Uplands: Book of the Courel and other poems*. tr. EM. El Paso: Veliz Books, 2020, 46. Used with permission.

51

Bishop, Elizabeth. "Questions of Travel," *POEMS*, op. cit., 91.

54

Bernlef, J. "A Conversation with Elizabeth Bishop," *Conversations with Elizabeth Bishop*, ed. George Monteiro. Jackson: U Press of Mississippi, 1976, 62.

Hartley, L. P. *The Go-Between* (1953). NYC: Penguin Classics, 2011. This quote's been in my head since I saw the film in 1971; it is the first line of the book.

In a letter, 21 March 1972 (in *One Art*, op. cit.), EB urged Robert Lowell against publishing *The Dolphin* (1973), with its use of letters from his ex-wife: "One can use one's life as material [for poems]—one does anyway—but these letters—aren't you violating a trust? IF you were given permission—IF you hadn't changed them ... etc. But *art just isn't worth that much*."

Robbins, Tom. "Now Playing: A Touch of the Poetess," *Seattle Magazine*, April 1966.

56

Cleghorn, Angus, with Bethany Hicok and Thomas Travisano. *Elizabeth Bishop in the Twenty-First Century: Reading the New Editions*. Charlottesville: U Virginia Press, 2012, 183. *Reference to Robert Lowell and his luminism comment.

Bishop, Elizabeth. Letter to May Swensen, 3 July 1958, in *One Art*, op. cit., 361.

58

EM poem imitates Bishop's "Filling Station," which is in *POEMS*, op.cit., 125.

61

Brant, Alice Dayrell Caldeira. *Diary of "Helena Morley,"* tr. Elizabeth Bishop from *Minha Vida de Meninha*, 1942. NYC: Farrar, Straus and Cudahy, 1957.

62

Bishop, Elizabeth. From a letter to Anne Stevenson, 8 January 1964, quoted in *Elizabeth Bishop: Life and the Memory of It*, by Brett C. Millier. Berkeley: U California Press, 1993, 352. The letter is in the Elizabeth Bishop papers, Washington University in St. Louis Library.

64

Bishop, Elizabeth. "Letter to Anne Stevenson, 16 February 1964," *PROSE*. NYC: Farrar, Straus and Giroux, 2015, 421. Here B refers to the poem as "fausse naïve."

65

Herbert, George. "Love Unknown." Herbert was a Welsh metaphysical poet of the early 17th century. Poem available online.

Newspaper references from *Luta Democrática*, Rio de Janeiro, 21 January 1964, 1–2.

68

Moure, Erín. *Kapusta: A play-poem-ash*. Toronto: House of Anansi, 2015.

Iris Turcott https://www.canadiantheatre.com/dict.pl?term=Turcott%2C%20Iris.

69

Rilke, Rainer Maria. "Archaic Torso of Apollo," op. cit.

70–71

Drummond de Andrade, Carlos. "Poema de Sete Faces," *Drummond: Antologia Poética.* Rio de Janeiro: Olimpia Editora, 1962, 3.

EM transalteration "7-Sided Poem." Bishop's translation available online.

72

On Bishop's last house: Rivas, Fátima Cristina, with Filipe de Oliveira Correio, Jacqueline de Cassia, P. Lima Correio, Idemburgo Pereira Frazão Félix Correio, "O Sentimento de Não-Pertencimento da Poeta Elizabeth Bishop," https://1library.org/document/zlnvlngq-sentimento-de-nao-pertencimento-da-poeta-elizabeth-bishop.html; *"Ainda, segundo impressões do seu tradutor, encontradas no livro* Poemas Escolhidos de Elizabeth Bishop *(2012), a poetisa, no final de sua vida, remontando ás lembranças do Brasil, comprou e decorou um apartamento no porto de Boston com muitos artefatos e peças brasileiras, entre carrancas do Rio São Francisco até santos e ex-votos. EB, inclusivo, mudava as roupas dos santos de acordo com as festividades no Brasil."*

Saddle shoes were a mark of class too, as I recall: how I envied them! https://www.keikari.com/english/a-history-of-saddle-shoes/.

Phrases from Bishop are extracted from her letters, *One Art,* op. cit.

73

Collaged phrases are lines from Bishop, extracted from her letters, *One Art,* op. cit.

74

Bishop often signed her letters "Abraços e saudades," *hugs and remembrance-longings.*

75

Grimké, Angelina Weld. Quote from an uncollected version of a poem that exists in other versions in her *Selected Works*, found in "Angelina Weld Daughter of Archibald Grimke" (2017), manuscripts for the Grimke Book, 32. http://dh.howard.edu/ajc_grimke_manuscripts/32.

76

Scott, Julius S. *The Common Wind: Afro-American Currents in the Age of the Haitian Revolution.* NYC: Verso Books, 2018, 81.

77

Laclau, Ernesto, and Chantal Mouffe. *Hegemony and Socialist Strategy*. London: Verso, 1985. (re constitutive outside)

Glissant, Édouard. "On Opacity," *Poetics of Relation*, tr. Betsy Wing. Ann Arbor: U Michigan Press, 1990, 244.

Bhabha, Homi. *Les lieux de la culture : une théorie postcoloniale*, tr. Françoise Bouillot. Paris: Payot & Rivages, 2019, 2e éd. (French edition of *The Location of Culture*), 418.

78

*Moure, Eirin. *Sheep's Vigil by a Fervent Person: A Transelation of Alberto Caeiro/ Fernando Pessoa's O Guardador de Rebahnhos*. Toronto: House of Anansi, 2001, 2004, 123.

79

Agamben, Giorgio. *Profanations*. Tr. Jeff Fort. Princeton, NJ: Princeton U Press, 2005, 67.

80

Grimké, Angelina Weld. "Rachel," *Selected Works of Angelina Weld Grimké*. NYC and London: Oxford U Press, 1991, 123.

Roberts, Brian Russell. *Artistic Ambassadors: Literary and International Representation of the New Negro Era*. Charlottesville: U Virginia Press, 2013, 93.

81

Arendt, Hannah. "Vita activa," ch. 1, *The Human Condition*. Chicago: U Chicago Press, 1958.

Kant, Immanuel. *Critique of Judgment*. Tr. W. S. Pluhar. Indianapolis: Hackett, 1987, 52.

Hölderlin, Friedrich. "Wir lernen nichts schwerer als das Nationelle frei gebrauchen." The hardest to learn is the "Nationelle," i.e. that which is ours by birth (nature, vs. culture). Much discussion of this in Heidegger, and Chus Pato picks it up in her *At the Limit* (tr. EM from *Baixo o límite*, RAG 2017, online), Montreal: Zat-So Productions, 2018.

Pato, Chus. *Un libre favor*. Vigo: Galaxia, 2016. tr. by EM as *The Face of the Quartzes*. El Paso: Veliz Books, 2021.

Martí, José, and Máximo Gómez. *Montecristi Manifesto*. 1895. Available online.

83

Archibald H. Grimke Papers. Moorland-Spingarn Research Center, Howard U, Washington, DC. https://huaspace.wrlc.org/public/repositories/2/resources/357.

History of family and brothers: https://bostonathenaeum.org/blog/archibald-henry-grimke/:

"With the unexpected death of his father in 1860, Archibald and his brother Francis were returned to slavery to work as servants at his half-brother, E. Montague Grimké's house. Henry wanted Nancy and her children to be treated as part of the family but unfortunately that wish was not honored by E. Montague. In 1863 Archibald escaped his half-brother's house and spent that last year of the Civil War in hiding. Francis was sold to a Confederate Officer and had to wait for the war to end before gaining his freedom. After the war Archibald attended the Freedmen's Bureau's newly created Morris Street School, then Lincoln University at Pennsylvania in 1867 where he earned a bachelor's in 1870 and a master's in 1872."

Grimké, Sarah Stanley. *Personified Unthinkables: An Argument Against Physical Causation.* Michigan, 1884. Online.

84

Grimké, Sarah Stanley. Her letters to AWG in Box 5, Folder 92, Angelina Weld Grimké papers, Manuscript Division, Moorland-Spingarn Research Center, Howard University, Washington, DC.

Honey, Maureen. *Aphrodite's Daughters. Three Modernist Poets of the Harlem Renaissance.* Rutgers, NJ: Rutgers U Press, 2016, 77. Excellent account of AWG's life.

85

Scott, Julius S. *The Common Wind*, op. cit. Condensed here in the last paragraph are my takeaways from this and other books but primarily from this one.

86

Grimké, Sarah Stanley. *First Lessons in Reality.* Michigan, 1886. Online.

88

Grimké, Angelina Weld. "Evanescence," *Selected Works*, op.cit., 66.

89

Grimké, Angelina Weld. "Dawn (2)," *Selected Works*, op. cit., 77, and from "El Beso," op. cit., 82.

Kerlin, Robert T., ed. *Negro Poets and their Poems*. Washington, DC: Associated Publishers, 1923.

Locke, Alain, ed. *The New Negro*. NYC: Atheneum, 1925.

Hughes, Langston, and Arna Bontemps, eds. *Poetry of the Negro, 1746–1949: An Anthology.* Garden City, NY: Doubleday, 1949.

93

Arendt, Hannah. *The Human Condition*, op. cit.

94

Grimké, Angelina Weld. "The Black Finger," *Selected Works*, op. cit., 101.

96

Villarreal, Rebecca. "On Angelina Weld Grimké." Online. https://washingtonart.com/beltway/grimke.html. Accessed 14 April 2023.

Grimké, Angelina Weld. from "Evanescence," op. cit.

97

*Moure, Erín. From "Hundreds dropped …" *The Elements*, op. cit., 5.

100

Pato, Chus. from "O natal para o poema," phrase tr. EM. Online. https://euseino.org/2019/10/14/chus-pato-sobre-o-estado-da-poesia/.

103

Arendt, Hannah. *The Human Condition*, op. cit.
Bhabha, Homi. *The Location of Culture*, op. cit., 37.

104

Bhabha, Homi. op. cit., 37. *Same quote as the image-text on 103, where it was created by a machine (a damaged scan).*

105

Grimké, Angelina Weld. Tr. EM from "Futility (2)," *Selected Works*, op. cit., 107.

111

Spivak, Gayatri Chakravorty. "The Left Reflects on the Global Pandemic and Speaks to Transform!!" *Journal of Bioethical Inquiry* 17, no. 4 (September 2020). https://www.ncbi.nlm.nih.gov/pmc/articles/PMC7651809/.

113

de Castro, Rosalia. "Alborada," from *Cantares Gallegos*, 1863, tr. EM in *Galician Songs*. Sofia, Bulgaria: Small Stations Press, 2016, 165. Used with permission.

125

Epigraph from Italian anaesthesiologist Annalisa Silvestriana during first wave of Covid-19 in Italy, 2020, documented by photographer Alberto Giuliani, in his series *San Salvatore*: https://scotiabankcontactphoto.com/alberto-giuliani-san-salvatore/annalisa-silvestrianaesthesiologist/ "Before I put them to sleep and intubate them, I have them make a phone call to a relative. A greeting, to tell each other that all will go well. But it's not so. And so it happens that the relatives, in tears, ask us to be close to their family member, to caress them, and to tell them—even if they cannot hear us—that they loved them, that they will miss them. This is the final greeting, which we bring every day."

130

Guzman, Coco. *The Demonstration*, MAI, Montreal, 6 October–12 November 2016. https://www.burningbillboard.art/coco-guzman-the-demonstration/.

133

A 'work of literature' occurs not on the page but between reader and page, a third space. A translator cannot help but imbue their own body in what they translate, for we can only translate what we read. Reading is always contemporary; even a text ancient and opaque comes 'alive' in that third space, which is always actual. A text in itself is a non-breath; without the breath of the reader, Quintilian lies dormant in the archive. Thus George Floyd imbues an outcry in a text on asthma from 1985 read today. The original poem (*Domestic Fuel*, Toronto: Anansi, 1985, 104) says: "I can't breathe." Here the poem is revised to read: "I can't breath_*" as asthma no longer owns that sentence, and must recognize police violence, including murder of Black people, Black men, Black children of Black mothers who have hopes for them and love them. If the poem is free, bears freedom, and I believe it can do this, it must give itself over to speech itself, and go silent. This too is a mode of translation.

138
Vallejo, César. *Trilce.* 1922. https://www.britannica.com/biography/Cesar-Vallejo#ref205417: "In 1920 Vallejo's involvement in political matters concerning Indians led to his imprisonment for nearly three months. This experience heightened his feeling of loss at the death of his mother and contributed to a state of depression that was to torment him the rest of his life. *Escalas melografiadas* (1922; "Musical Scales"), a collection of short stories, and many of the more complex poems of *Trilce* (1922; Eng. tr. *Trilce*) were conceived during his imprisonment. In his major work *Trilce*, Vallejo signaled his complete break with tradition by incorporating neologisms, colloquialisms, typographic innovations, and startling imagery, with which he sought to express the disparity that he felt existed between human aspirations and the limitations imposed on people by biological existence and social organization."

144
Bhabha, Homi. *Les lieux de la culture : une théorie postcoloniale.* Op. cit., 430.

REMERCIEMENTS

Alligatorzine (May 2020; thanks Rachel Blau Duplessis), *Brooklyn Rail* (April 2020; thanks Norma Cole), *Âllo-poème Montréal* (December 2020; thanks Sébastien Dulude), *Vallejo & Co.* (thanks Andrés Ajens), www.vallejoandcompany.com/trilce-xxxii-por-erin-moure, Small Stations Press re Rosalía de Castro's *Galician Songs* (2016). Veliz Books re Uxío *Novoneyra's The Uplands: Book of the Courel and other poems* (2020).

Thanks to Christina Davis and the Woodberry Poetry Room at Harvard University for the Creative Fellowship (April 2017) that enabled my initial research and pulled me into this rabbit hole for six years!

Thanks to Rachel Blau Duplessis for early encouragement, Oana Avasilichioaei for first editing and ongoing encouragement, Robert Majzels for acute editorial questioning of my contradictions, Oana and my brother Ken for access to university library materials shut to scholars outside the institution. Merci à Chantal Neveu pour nos conversations si riches, and to Kim Fullerton for drawings and problem-solving in life in general.

Thanks to Norma Cole for her unwavering example of poetry, language, translation, compassion, patience, justice, health.

Special thanks to Hoa Nguyen whose astute editorial eye and questions were indispensable to spur my final shaping and revisions.

Special thanks to Karis Shearer who lent me her *Collected* Bishop for all the years it took, and maybe I haven't given it back yet … and for her support and ear.

Thanks to PennSound for the voice of Muriel Rukeyser, and to a 1977 film by Richard O. Moore that captures her in movement.

Thanks to U Winnipeg and Sandy Pool for inviting me as Jake MacDonald Writer in Residence (virtual) in Fall 2021, giving me precious time to work on this book.

Grazas to Chus Pato for her *At the Limit* and *Un libre favor* (*The Face of the Quartzes* in English) and who, via her thinking on natality and the proper, gave fuel to my consideration of Grimké's natality-fecundity conundrum.

Thanks to the 21st century for breath: Oxese™ (formoterol fumarate dihydrate), Pulmicort™ (budesonide), Singulair™ (montelukast, a leukotriene receptor antagonist), Zithromax™ (azithromycin), Benadryl™ (diphenhydramine hydrochloride), EpiPen™ (epinephrine or adrenaline), Guaifenesin (glyceryl guaiacolate). I remember the 20th century and it was not fun.

Thanks to public health care (Canada); it's not perfect but has enabled me to make a life in poetry outside universities and companies.

Big thanks to Laurie Gunn, and Elizabeth Bishop House, Great Village, Nova Scotia, where on a week's residency in June 2022, I responded to Hoa's first questions, on Mi'kmaw shores dyked 300 years ago by Acadian settlers to drain marshes for agriculture. Charles and Marie (Bourque) Robichaud settled here in 1720 to farm amid the Mi'kmaq; they and others were deported by the British in 1755–64 and their homes burned, and fields given to British settlers. Acadian place names—French spellings of Mi'kmaw names—were kept by the British, i.e. Cobequid Bay (We'kopekwitk) and Economy (Économie, for Kenomee: where land juts into sea, or 'point,' thus Economy Point is redundant). Acadians were later allowed back to the colonies but not Nova Scotia. Bishop's English ancestors settled later, as townspeople and tradespersons, though theirs had elements of farming life (a cow!). The migrations of peoples, their exclusion, ethnic cleansing, genocide, is layered multiply on this Mi'kmaw red earth. Did EB know the Acadian history? To my knowledge, she made no mention of it or of the Mi'kmaq or the lands of Mi'kma'qi. But time's threshold is different now, so it needs to be said.

Agradecementos ao idioma galego que me permite ler en portugués e en brasileiro.

TEXTS AND PRESENCES 2016-2023 NOT IN ENDNOTES

Benjamin, Walter. "The Task of the Translator," for its passages and relation to Glissant/Martí's archipelago. In many translations (see p. 163).
Harris, Claire. *The Conception of Winter* (1989), *Drawing Down a Daughter* (1992), *Fables from the Women's Quarters* (1984). I have tried to be true to what I was taught, and am still sorry for my insolence.

Read on/by/for Rukeyser

Muriel Rukeyser, *The Green Wave.* I bought a copy of this 1948 book because it's vital to read books in their original conception. A beautiful revelation.
"The Speed of Darkness," a poem once a personal touchstone and now troubling to me: https://www.poetryfoundation.org/poems/56287/the-speed-of-darkness. Rukeyser read this poem in Montreal (and "Elegy in Joy" too) at Sir George Williams University on 24 January 1969. https://montreal.spokenweb.ca/sgw-poetry-readings/muriel-rukeyser-at-sgwu-1969/.
Jane Malcolm's article on Rukeyser and the poetry reading, online at *Amodern*, quotes Kate Daniels's "Muriel Rukeyser and Her Literary Critics" from *Gendered Modernisms: American Women Poets and Their Readers*, ed. Margaret Dickie and Thomas Travisano. Philadelphia: U Penn Press, 1996, 257.
Galway Kinnell on one of Rukeyser's last readings: https://aprweb.org/poems/jubilate1.
Kinnell and Sharon Olds on Rukeyser (Kinnell reading MR words on Whitman, from *The Life of Poetry*) https://www.youtube.com/watch?v=UDFbtsJzRXo.

Read on/by/for Bishop

http://elizabethbishopcentenary.blogspot.com.
https://www.tibordenagy.com/exhibitions/elizabeth-bishop.
Green, Fiona. "Elizabeth Bishop in Brazil and the New Yorker" *Journal of American Studies*, 46 (2012), 803–29. Read after this book was done but reinforced my readings, as did Sandeep Parmar, "Race," in *Elizabeth Bishop in Context*, ed. A. Cleghorn and J. Ellis. Cambridge, UK: Cambridge U Press, 2021, 335–46.
Ferreira, Isabel Cristina Rodrigues, *The Dialogue About 'Racial Democracy' Among African-American And Afro-Brazilian Literatures.* PhD Dissertation, Chapel Hill U, 2008, for more on the "myth of racial democracy" re Brazil and USA.
de Jesus, Carolina Maria. *Quarto de Despejo: Diário dum favelada.* Rio de Janeiro, 1960, 10th ed. São Paulo: Ática, 2014. A much more interesting diary than the one

translated by Bishop (thanks to Hoa Nguyen for the clue). In the 1960s, her book outsold Clarice Lispector and Jorge Amado, her white contemporaries. On favelas and decolonization: https://wikifavelas.com.br.

Rodrigues, Douglas Lima, and Elisabete da Silva Barbosa. "O processo criativo do poema 'The Burglar of Babylon' a partir de uma abordagem sociocrítica" https://1library.org/document/zx0441oz-o-processo-criativo-do-poema-the-burglar-of-babylon-a-partir-de-uma-abordagem-sociocritica.html: *"No Brasil, a escritora frequentava espaços privilegiados, onde conviva com autoridades políticas, escritores e pessoas da alta sociedade brasileira (especialmente de inclinação mais à direita) por intermédio de sua companheira, Maria Carlota Costallat de Macedo Soares, mais conhecida como Lota."*

https://mulherias.blogosfera.uol.com.br/2020/09/11/o-legado-do-best-seller-quarto-de-despejo-na-vida-de-mulheres-negras/ in which: "o *epistemicídio*, termo que define o apagamento intelectual das contribuições africanas e indígenas ..."

Read on/by/for Grimké

Selected Works of AWG does not list dates of poems, so here are some, from *Radicals, Volume 1: Fiction, Poetry, and Drama: Audacious Writings by American Women, 1830–1930* (2021): "To Theodore Weld on His 90th Birthday" (1893), "Longing" (1901), "Beware Lest He Awakes" (1902), "El Beso" (1909), "To Keep the Memory of Charlotte Forten Grimké" (1915), "To the Dunbar High School" (1917), *Rachel* (produced 1916, 1921), "The Closing Door" (1919), *Rachel: A Play in Three Acts* (1920), "The Black Finger" (*Opportunity*, 1923), "The Want of You" (1923), "Trees" (*Carolina Magazine*, 1928), "At April" (*Opportunity*, 1925).

Johnson, K. Paul. "The Early Theosophical Society and the Hermetic Brotherhood of Lexor," June 2012. 11:37–15:18 are mentions of Sarah Stanley. https://www.youtube.com/watch?v=jn2Dz3pbXJ0.

Honey, Maureen, and Venetria K. Patton, eds. *Double-Take: A Revisionist Harlem Renaissance Anthology*. Rutgers, NJ: Rutgers U Press, 2001.

Anna Julia Cooper Collection; Howard University, Washington, DC, https://dh.howard.edu/ajcooper/

Mulich, Jeppe. *In a Sea of Empires: Networks and Crossings in the Revolutionary Caribbean*. Cambridge, UK: Cambridge U Press, 2020.

Grimké, Sarah Stanley. *Collected Works*, ed. K. Paul Johnson, 2019. Online. (works are in public domain)

https://library.brown.edu/create/modernlatinamerica/chapters/chapter-4-cuba/primary-documents-w-accompanying-discussion-questions/document-8-montecristi-manifesto-jose-marti-and-maximo-gomez-1895/.

https://www.poetryfoundation.org/poets/georgia-douglas-johnson.

Rankine, Claudia. *Just Us: An American Conversation*. Minneapolis: Graywolf, 2020.
Hong, Cathy Park. "Delusions of Whiteness in the Avant-Garde" in *Lana Turner Journal*, 2014 and online https://arcade.stanford.edu/content/delusions-whiteness-avant-garde, and Hong's books of poetry, which drew me to her essays.
Yusoff, Kathryn. *A Billion Black Anthropocenes or None*. Minneapolis: U Minnesota Press, 2018.

Read/watched during editing, May–June 2022

BBC Panorama, 2021: *"I Can't Breathe": Black and Dead in Custody*, dir. Calum McKay, https://www.youtube.com/watch?v=ybyQ1G9XTnM.
Mackey, Nathaniel. "Sound and Sentiment, Sound and Symbol," *Callaloo*, issue 30 (Winter 1987), pp. 29–54. https://www.jstor.org/stable/2930634. Online.
Boaventura de Sousa Santos. *The End of the Cognitive Empire: The Coming of Age of Epistemologies of the South*. Durham, NC: Duke U Press, 2018.

Read/watched as T was typeset November 2022 into 2023

Clarke, Chris. "The Complex Figure of the Poet–Translator as Exemplified by the Case of Muriel Rukeyser and Octavio Paz." Read in ms.
Glissant, Édouard. *La Cohée du Lamentin*. Paris: Gallimard, 2005.
Simic, Charles. "The Power of Reticence." Review of Elizabeth Bishop's *Edgar Allan Poe & the Jukebox: Uncollected poems, Drafts, and Fragments* (NY-FSG 2006), NYRB, April 27, 2006. An excellent description of EB and what she did in poems, for those who need an intro.

NEW YORK TIMES OBITUARIES

MR NYT quarter page, 13 February 1980 (died 12 February): **Muriel Rukeyser, Poet of Protest, Dies; A Definitive Line Traveled in Europe Wrote Children's Books**
"Muriel Rukeyser, whose poetry spanned four decades and rang with strong protests against inhumanity wherever she saw it, died yesterday afternoon at the East Side home of her literary agent and close friend, Monica McCall."

EB NYT quarter page, 8 October 1979, Section B, p. 13 (died 7 October) by Helen Vendler: **Elizabeth Bishop: Won a Pulitzer for Poetry and Taught at Harvard**
"Elizabeth Bishop, a Pulitzer Prize-winning poet who wrote sparingly but was lavishly praised for the elegance and precision with which she evoked the natural world, died of a ruptured cerebral aneurism Saturday at her home in Boston. She was 68 years old."

AWG NYT just two inches of one column, 11 June 1958, p. 36 (died 10 June): **Angelina W. Grimke, Poet, Ex Teacher, 78** (no free text access)

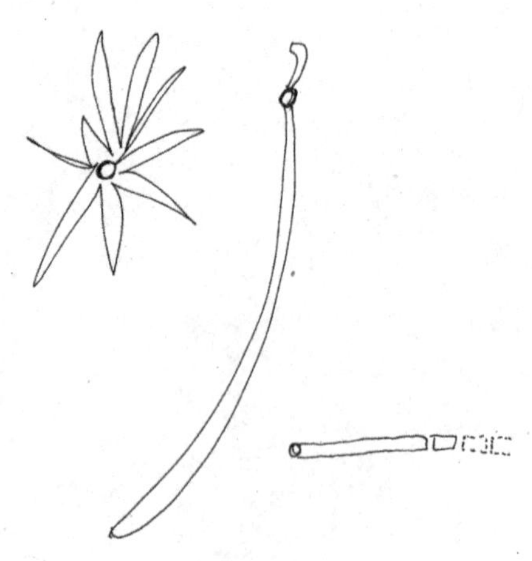

Rukeyser, Bishop, Grimké (Moure, 2019)

DIE AUFGABE DES ÜBERSETZERS

Curiously, Walter Benjamin's classic essay *on translation*, originally his introduction to his own translations from French of Baudelaire, is usually read *in translation*. In English it is known as "The Task of the Translator," but it could be:

The Act-respons-ability-gift of the Over-typesetters
(translation as pharmakon)

Eben darum wohnt in ihnen vor andern die ungeheure und ursprüngliche Gefahr aller Übersetzung: daß die Tore einer so erweiterten und durchwalteten Sprache zufallen und den Übersetzer ins Schweigen schließen. (Benjamin)

Precisamente por iso habita nelas o inmenso e orixinario perigo de toda tradución máis ca en ningunha outra: que as portas dunha lingua así expandida e completamente gobernada se fechen encerrando a quen traduce no silencio. (tr. Baltrusch, Garrido Vilariño, Montero Küpper)

C'est précisément pourquoi ses traductions [celles de Hölderlin, de Pindar] sont hantées comme nulle autre par le profond péril originel attaché à toute traduction : que les portes d'une langue si élargie et si maîtrisée ne retombent et n'enferment le traducteur dans le silence. (tr. Lamy, Nouss)

For this very reason, Hölderlin's *Pindar* harbours like no other the immense and originary danger of all translation: that the gates of a language so expanded and so fully controlled may fall shut and enclose the translator in silence. (tr. Moure)

leaving (*to you, dear reader, dearest trout*):

language itself

n a- r

Photograph credit: Elisa S.

ERÍN MOURE is a poet and translator (primarily of Galician and French poetry into English) who welcomes texts that are unconventional or difficult because she loves and needs them. Among other honours, she is a two-time winner of Canada's Governor General's Award (in poetry and translation), a winner of the Pat Lowther Memorial Award and the Nelson Ball Prize, a co-recipient of the QWF Spoken Word Prize, a three-time finalist for a Best Translated Book Award in poetry, and a three-time finalist for the Griffin Poetry Prize. She is based in Tiohtià:ke/Montreal.

ELISA SAMPEDRÍN is undependable. Her presence, like that of the shoe, worries the book.